DATE DUE

Demco, Inc. 38-293

JAN 1 2 2010

New & Selected Poems

AHSAHTA PRESS

The New Series

NUMBER 25

New & Selected Poems

Charles O. Hartman

Boise State University • Boise • Idaho • 2008

Ahsahta Press, Boise State University
Boise, Idaho 83725
http://ahsahtapress.boisestate.edu

Printed in the United States of America
Cover design by Quemadura
Author photo by Janet Hayes
Book design by Janet Holmes
First printing September 2008
ISBN-13: 978-1-934103-02-9

Library of Congress Cataloging-in-Publication Data

Hartman, Charles O., 1949–
[Poems. Selections]
New & selected poems / Charles O. Hartman.
    p. cm.—(The new series ; no. 25)
Includes index.
ISBN-13: 978-1-934103-02-9 (pbk. : alk. paper)
ISBN-10: 1-934103-02-0 (pbk. : alk. paper)
I. Title. II. Title: New and selected poems.
PS3558.A7116A6 2008
811'.54—DC22
                                        2007047289

Reach for the thing that will make the moment shine.
—GEORGE BENSON

ACKNOWLEDGMENTS

The author would like to thank the editors of the following publications, in which these
poems originally appeared: *Ascent, Common Knowledge, Field, Ironwood, Jacket, New American
Writing, Orpheus, Pleiades, Ploughshares, Poetry, Quarterly West, Temblor, Triquarterly, Tyuonyi,
Yale Review.* Many of these poems appeared in the author's earlier books *The Pigfoot Rebellion*
(1982), published by Godine Press; *True North* (1990), published by Copper Beech Press; *Glass
Enclosure* (1995) and *The Long View* (1999), published by Wesleyan University Press; and *Island*
(2004), published by Ahsahta Press. They are reprinted with permission of the copyright
holder.

CONTENTS

New Poems

Maybe So

We have a little time here
and are so small it can seem endless.
We begin by seeing the light, which is too bright,
and end in seeing it go too dim. Between,
—well, between we have jobs and babies,
opinions, loads of opinions. We have friends,
lovers, and we learn how little our opinions mean
because of them. We discover fear
and take years to grow intrigued by it,
find out how live we are on the edge of the bridge.
We discover love and recognize it as fear.
Between, we ask what the agenda is.
The agenda is the end. Never mind. And the light,
every day from its beginning and ours, sometimes more
and sometimes less, comes back to begin us over.
Just when we think we knew the front yard's routine
arrives the cardinal, two, the bright tangerine of her beak
the only thing in the world her wide eyes can't see,
the pick of his pert chirp slung over and over
at the rock-face of the morning, that blank chert
he exposes garnets in. We shake our heads
and go off to work, because work is what we do,
and that is its definition. You know this.
I know that. We have a little time here. We stockpile
batteries and pens, saxophone reeds for some,
for others sheep—it's all to the good.
They tell us it won't count. We know
what counts. Maybe it's even
because of all we've done
that a kiss comes in the middle of an afternoon,
not a new kiss if that means new lips,
new shoulders rounded into our awkward arms,
but still: a kiss that stops time for us, stops us
short on the bridge as if it had got rid
finally of its end and its beginning.
We remember that. Even at the end,
we remember that beginning, when the light
looked over our shoulder
and made us memorize every leaf, every feather,
every fear we came to love with, and the love.

THE CORECTIONS

I

Idealist, I dwell
      for hours in Photoshop
           on moving the chair

beside the statue where it should have been.
      In the sweet,
           the editable world

of integers that incandesce as color
      in a tissue of small cells
           and the instruments to doctor them,

a blemish is a choice.
      This wash of white,
           the wall, used to include the gray

hatch of a fuse box. Now light falls
      clean from the upper left like Day
           One and meets the hard

edge of the chair's right arm,
      as the first sight
           of Beatrice reached Dante.

Struck him, we say.
      She died. He was free
           to compose heaven around her.

II

This light so revels through the blue
glass of the bottle and its years-

sere still barely yellow jonquils
within the snow scene shining through the wide

casement, it's worth the time
to work on the window screen, the seasons

of crud stuck in its "interstices
between the intersections":

to pick from the grid a pure vacuity
with the right tone of snowlight behind it

to copy, one by one
replacing each congested cell.

Later I might scrub
the physical one. But why?

Wise lively sleep,
to revise the dead.

III
This note that there
    was wrong I moved
        here in place of
            a mistake I played

Now it sounds right
    so it is
        This word wrong there
            I moved here to

make right a mistake
    I spoke last night
        as you will recall
            as I surely do

IV

Nation in the hands of god-rabid thugs?
Vote!

—the pixel feels in its heart it is
"just the wrong shade of pinky-russet"

Being green
in a sunset will not do

Photographs never lie
about photons

There was no headline in the sky
and now there is

V

During one step toward the stairs,
        to recall first the forgotten robe,
                then that the shortest path
back to the bathroom isn't back
        but forward around the hall,

            makes for a hitch
in the step but the step
        gets made. "Between
            the essence and the descent"
flow—like frames, if frames could flow

        (and they can make one)—two or three
          decisions, each
room enough to turn
      around in like an ox
        in a warm stall.

VI

When Dante in his dream first speaks with Beatrice
he is still in Purgatory.
                              He calls her voice
a sword.
              She bathes him
in Lethe, and he swallows its waters.
                                        All this time
naturally he would be writing notes to himself,
except that he is writing the poem in which it happens.

He will have been sitting at a desk by a window lattice,
or walking the fields near Florence, if he was not
already in exile, I can't remember.
                                      He dreams Beatrice
onto paper as he had begun dreaming back
in the *Vita Nuova*, when she died.
                                      He devotes
a whole canto to correcting, to having her correct
the life he has lived between,
                                in this book between
the two that picture the From and hopeful To,
the books everybody remembers best,
                                      which is odd
since this is the one we live in.

PETTING ZOO

Spring: the edges and middles
of these roads blossom
with corpses, racoon, possum, crow-

lunch, bodies bloomed rosy
into meat and gut, colors
saturated. Eye catching

until the eye learns better.
The slow skunk
lingers in brief afterlife

either because the tail sacs
burst on impact
or because it tried

to warn off what was coming.
Pond-turtle crushed to lotus.
Last week the fox flung itself

under my fender—Last week
I hit a fox—Last week my car—
I could make this a poem

about old lovers. I do
worry, slowing down and then
farther down, about being

able to get anywhere.
The thoughtful driver watches
out at all times, maintaining

an easy and natural grip.
I check my fluids weekly,
night after night dream a dim

on-ramp crowded with faint
shapes, fur thick behind
the ears, under my fingers,

my lights, while the back legs jerk
a couple of times. I don't
see for the life of me

how I'd ever end that poem.
My species is all crazy,
think of it, mammals with wheels.

CATCH A PIGEON

and put it head first in your coat pocket.

It will think night has fallen and keep still.
When you get it home give it some nectar

and teach it to beg for food by fixing
whoever comes in with its ochre eye,
holding out one claw; it will take a while

to achieve the appropriate balance.
Let it have half the food. After a year
pick a honey-lemon-yellow Sunday;

on the table in the breakfast nook, first
break its neck with the dictionary, then
slit it open and hunt around inside.

The entrails won't mean anything to you
but you might like the tiny cameo

preserving every detail of your face.

COURT

§

Once dawn gets going
pigeons race by madcap. Gang creatures early.
What do they see
in a high hurry?

§

On the balcony across, above left: aluminum walker. Never moved. From the door to one side of it emerges a man carrying a grudge, a grumble in his fist. Through the other, sometimes, glimpses of a schoolgirl who squirms at her cramped desk. Often a trim woman with competent gray hair dusting the railing, hanging underwear, sheets that stay for days.

§

What is the question, they ask, suspending you eighty feet over the yard. Say two seconds. Say twenty-five meters per second. And the kingdoms thereof.

§

He is risen! Lord knows what for. Friends in high places.

§

Are pigeons interested in pigeonshit? Do they go through an anal phase? Does the power of flight determine the mythology of excrement? *Man he knows how to lighten his load—*

§

As for the flat across and down: three women wash the bejeezus out of it every day. No furniture to speak of. Immaculate parquet.

§

Principle of the light well: Minoan.
Principle of the balcony: Bauhaus, cantilever, rebar.
Law of the Uncovered: that seven per cent of every lot remain unbuilt. Push the bare backsides to the center, a tall hollow, a long block long and a short

wide. Taller than wide, twice as long as tall.
Principle of greening family space: the village.

§
The floor is neuter and the ceiling,
the walls masculine, the door
the door is feminine.

§
Birds you miss: redwing black, mocking, cat. But the high-perched ungain-
ly-tailed white-flaunting magpie speaks its moniker: *karakaxa*. Anywhere,
only these, of us all on and near the earth,
move in helices.

§
On the roofs
the ranks of antennas at attention to the sun rising
as it will
in the southeast listen
to their sectors of sky. The moon-ears cup
southwest toward theirs.

§
The seven-story apartment building. The five-paragraph essay. Athens'
hung gardens. Those shapely shrubberies. How is it that often some wellfed
mobile people don't think about sex?

§
Someone's alarm begins every seven a.m. Continues. Odds on they're out of
town. Buncha guys renovating the apartment up and to the right knock off
for everyone's two-thirty siesta. Sometimes. For the sake of the next genera-
tion, now in progress.

§
There it is again: stray
memory: not a hole in one's life
so much as an impacted spot.
My word this air comes thick with noises from the hidden mouths of noise.

§

Even here a trace of the old roofing, red fired clay half-pipes laid convex course over concave. In the village, the upturned tiles that drain rain away are called nuns, those that cover the gap between, priests.

§

Beyond the exigeant metal people of the roof: parallel contrails. Nobody plans these things, the products of planning. Nothing otherwise in the sky to mention, nothing to speak of.

§

A third of the Greeks in Greece have moved into Athens (but Melbourne, Chicago, Montreal). Back to the ancestral home to vote: a Sunday of silence. City of strangers. Ethnologists have something to say. Ethologists too. A pair of pigeons mates on the next landing,
two seconds' hump,
ten minutes pecking mites from each other's head,
nictating lid turned glaucous to the sky.
Mum. Da.

§

Every dwelling above the basement pierces the whole fabric. Through the apartment's length from street echoing down corridor angles to back balcony, a voice in the muzzy megaphone of a creeping pickup, the tone menace till word-memory kicks in: *Flowers, pots, very beautiful plants.*

§

You got off the #13 trolley with a fistful of flowers, lapels looking freshly brushed, but it's just these new fabrics. *Never properly introduced.*

§

A clause in the constitution of our sense of time
says we will barely see day creep
down the face of the western building,
gold over brown
just to the latch now
on the shutter three from the top.
Whoever's walker it is might see it better.

§

Forgot to mention the wall! A bedroom broad a building tall. Stucco nurses
a vine with a trunk at one bottom corner and the lattice of dry branches to
lace tightly the whole height like advanced circuitry. Not quite. The root
starts out of sight behind another wall down there in the ground's indeci-
pherable warren and the vine has a dozen meters to go to peter
out at the roof line
as it must
where sky takes over. Meanwhile between,
sparrows nest here: s.n.h.

§

Five apparently identical pairs of women's underwear droop along a line
beside the block's biggest dish, Nokia. Mitsubishi, says the air conditioner.
Many repeat this or its cousin Panasonic or their uncle Sanyo, a stray pair of
Carriers—but two high up say Trane, Trane. Promises, promises.

§

Thank God you said, weaving your wary curiosity through the market with
an eye for an olive, ear for an archaic dative, *thank god I'm a stranger*. Don'
know. Sense wants to be made. The vine. The walker.

§

Everybody's music, now and then. Giant
Steps.

§

Flats stacked in towers, towers ringing blocks, blocks articulating neighbor-
hoods, neighborhoods eating blindly into each other's archaic edges.

§

Some he is yelling at some her: subject, object. Voice is feminine. Hand is
neuter. The noun for lout is masculine and means
villager.

§

The police whine by overhead.

§

Wring the dirt out!

§

More birds. In the port's parking lot you watched the sailor-between-ships move from motorbike to motorbike peering into the teardrop mirrors to work his toothpick, one by one.

§

Light! Make us
light!

§

In the village this would be our square. *Good evening.* Here after dark you can walk out naked: where we hang our clothes, no clothes. Airs curl around us, curious and surer of our love than a saint of heaven.

§

Breeze is the luxury we need.

§

Things that billow: plastic over the unfinished windowframe; skirts; anony-mous white hung cloth. Outermost tendrils of bougainvillea from the pent-house, seven floors' munificent cascade, riffling in sunset. Things better fastened—leaves of potted ficus, heart, half-open shutter—tremble.

§

When we say *The child is beautiful* we remember
to spit two times to ward the Eye
open to everything. A word is heard.

§

The difference between a cleaning-woman and a cleaning woman begins with pay-structure. At dusk she is dusting the empty clothesline.

§

Whose home's here? Stranger is masculine you think. Family is feminine and means *house-people*. Neighbor you can't recall. A few hundreds around this one ragged well. Around, millions. Who's home here?

§

In twilight, *wolf-light*, a bat no bigger than a sparrow makes free of the whole cavern of it, savannah, entomo-arcade: sings it
down
to the millimeter.

WHAT TO DO WITH YOUR EYE

Run it over this mown field.
Move it or let it catch.
Lift it, cast it down.
Pass it over the abandoned
basket of green peppers
and one red. Train it without mercy
between rows
on the pecked sockets of the mouse.
Have one for horseflesh. Keep it
peeled. Believe it as you can.

Be up to it in debt.
Keep it on the ball.
Pluck it out if it offends
or pay with it for another.
Cry it out. Please it
and plague the heart.

Landscape with Marmots:
Quasimodo Unstraps His Hump

The sky today is a blue that makes other things
petition to be compared to it,
trees that reserved judgment through half May
riot out green all over to the cheers of birds,

the sore throat and the foreign war plead valid cases
almost in vain, and the bank balance
on its short chain forgets to threaten
with customary rancor.

Supposing out at the edge of each world
the rim of darkness lies (often invading
the center, the one place
that can produce it): what gives it that lie?

The very woodchuck of last week
works her way through the high halms now
with a dwarf double at her hungry side, aware
unconscious of the craft of foxes.

We for whom the hardest lesson is that no virtue
inheres in being uncomfortable or unhappy
may suffer on a day like this
the vertigo of a stair missed in the dark.

Easier to offer thanks for the afternoon
once we know we could not deserve it,
as when the hunter with the groundhog in his sights
decides gracefully never to have existed.

THE STRANGE

fungus raised by the night's rain
　　　　dreams in the day's lawn. Mist lifts.
　　　　　　　Up from the deck's timbers blooms
the other, astral body
　　　of the skunk who houses there,

　　　　　　a sweet familiar story.
After a scratch song on sex
　　　flung down from the wild cherry,
　　　　　　sampling gulls jays chipmunks and
the stuck windows of the world,

　　　　the catbird flits to the rail
　　　　　　and lights by the resting hand.
Who'd give this up by moving?
　　　Sun teases out tufts of cloud
　　　　　to wind on the sky spindle.

Things change by rungs and you bring
　　　a child to an altered world.
　　　　　　Then woman. Then gone. I'm so
big beside the trusting bird—
　　　slope patiently trodden up

　　　　　by a populace of gifts.
Witness the blue, decrepit,
　　　greasy cat in the guest room,
　　　　　marking time. Witness catnip
gone to such prodigal seed

　　　in the fallen flowerbox.
　　　　　She would have said, *the catnip,*
your catnip, with a mocking
　　　eye. It isn't that I don't
　　　　　remember, only that things

grow well beyond me. Alone,
         the dead oak whitens daily.
              Beetles in the winter cord
multiply like dragonflies
         over grass, like wishes. Look,

              bird—abroad in the daylight,
velvet scurry in a green
         thicket, a mole, darker than
              your gray shoulders and as soft.
What would we save ourselves for?

         remembering everything.
            Apparently, out of the
blue, in catbird morning, spores
         of fecund astonishment
              thread cubic miles of humus.

HAPPEN TO

Out here in time
a dog in her last days
stands when she can

close enough to touch
her friend for life, facing away;
the hindquarters quiver, the eyes

keep watch. *Things happen* means the mind
knows but can't
contain them. Too near

a woman drives to work,
the drunk truck veers,
the whole spine seizes

one more time. How far away
is it that a man strapped in
falls out of the sky with two hundred others

he's never met? Or again my father
squeezes the trigger? None of it happened
to me, except as in dreams,

dreams none of them
can wake from. I dream
a station where what we call

the untimely are sorted
from the timely. I am the land
where things keep happening;

the place where I keep them
happening, yet
Kathy can think of a crazy saving swerve

and Ruby who can't prance can worry
what will become of her
friend, the man keep falling toward the field,

my father load with his one hand,
my lover mouth
another name; the road

where she sleeps
at her own wheel,
where the car keeps burning.

THE MOTH SONG

The moths on the wall are dreaming of Zanzibar
Their heads all point to the ceiling
Their legs are hid under their folded wings
They listen to rain on the tambour skylight
Their weary mouth-parts rest on the plasterboard
They understand the value of patience
They understand the value of patience
The virtue of patience is very much on their minds

The men on the pier appear to be thinking of going away
Their eyes all point to the ocean
Their legs are crossed at the ankles
They listen to waves among tabla timbers
Their elbows have grown into the wood of the railing
They understand the value of freedom
They understand the value of freedom
The virtues attaching to freedom inform their plans

The rocks on the hill are dreaming in Portuguese
Their heads all point to the sky
Their legs are hid under their folded wings
They listen to springs in the rain-stick crevices
They hoard the cool of the earth in their bellies
They understand the value of solitude
They understand the value of solitude
The virtues of solitude illuminate their days

Transparent Animals

1. *Situation*
Out here, well
below the air, miles yet
above bottom,
far from the mud rim of the world

2. *Chemistry*
I frame my frame
mostly of gelatin
which being in-
organic passes
light. As
well shall I be
mostly water

3. *Holdings*
Suppose I make my gut, full of what
sustains and still
shows!
a thread
held as I move always
vertical to cast
least shadow

4. *Uncertainty*
The retinas
to take light
can't refuse it—
so I make them tiny with
glassy cables, or shall they be
far from my body on stalks, or no,
spread huge and vanishingly thin

5. *Catch*
My gonads willy-nilly will stand out

HOW WE SHINE

How does it go
        heart of mine
Haven't we grown
        to a strange
                design
Are you concerned
        are you resigned
Would you agree
        we know
                how to shine

Calendar walls
        brilliant dreams
When do we know
        what the day
                redeems
Have all our plans
        run to extremes
Is it as long
        till night
                as it seems

Betty and Jill
        Bill and Joe
over the hill
        and away
                they go
Whiskey and rain
        chocolate and snow
Nobody means
        to lose
                as you know

FLAMENCO SKETCHES: MILES

Still fall
Another drift of sunshine
A day, and then some
No need for snow

Strange creatures scaled down
We tune a canny ear to the unmoved hour

Strung high, the icy cloud sings of a blue trapped in a blue
And so: too

Off on one hand the rind of an undiscarded moon
Off-season fields lie paralyzed for some Persephone
Her place held firm by a zero
Between's return

Then again, the spring's wound one way

AS EVER

Now it is fallen
now it is sawn and hauled
but oh years
the dead tree thought

How long to stand here
bureau of snow
sun-blancher
jay station crow's nest

mottler in rain
no leaf to let drop
stripped to woodbone
limbs in perennial

shrug magnanimous eyesore
deep-seamed
hovering
cloud-white but hard cloud-

gray but rooted
only child
Come squirrel
scratch in a crotch

Take off these brambles
I took them *untwine the bittersweet*
woodbine and bullbriar
to heap at the splay foot

wildrose and old nylon
tendril of archaic hammock
till mowing could
include it in yard

Shall I take nothing
further from the earth
no green felicity
but mechanic fastness
convocation of politic beetles
Fill the granted ovoid
no criss-cross branch
touching another

take slate from storm-
sky and when wild turkey
plumped on the lever end
of a happy

happy bough
how you jiggled then
rocked then held
unflagging fencer

extended to utmost
in final form
Bird and chipmunk
and beings in bonehouse
keep weirdly
coming and going
we do
How can you know

how to be same
hour to hour
After it fell
all the morning

all up and down
starlings perched
as happily
as ever

In Focus

personal density is inversely proportional
to temporal bandwidth

—Th. Pynchon

In a half-remembered place
at every next turn might appear
a scene real both ways, as
geometry and smell.
Oh yes! says the self.
Bearings. Tautology
caught by the corners.
That's the mind: *not this, the next.*

What appeared
when we first said the word *appear*
was angels. The old,
got loose, get lost, and experts ask,
right handed or left?
We bear where we tend.
What I've done I do. Within a hair,
all species are extinct.
Hardly worth recalling which one's mine.
So the mind
quails while the spirit
soars because that's all the spirit knows,
which explains how
little use mind has for spirit, too,
so we made the self to speak both ways,
a woman with two lovers,

proving that no one
can be saying this. Where was I?
Is this the street, or was that
a different city, another
decade, a door
I closed with the left hand,
keys in the right,
so many times?

A WALK IN WINTER

I think it is winter, afternoon.
My father and I walk
in pine woods in jackets
too thin for the wind
and don't talk about the war
we never talk about, the shells,
the minefield he woke in, stumbling
on enemy, the fire he called down
on his position. The needles
mute our steps, our hands
bunch in their pockets.
It must be New Hampshire,
our dark north, though the ocean
of his last home salts the air too
in our mouths. We come out
on a field of husks
waiting for spring
which will make no difference.
We have agreed without
having argued. The ocean is silent,
the trees say hardly anything,
on the far edge birds contend.
Suddenly I'm shouting *Don't you*
understand, I only get one father.
He smiles his hard-worn
comprehensive smile—
some photos remember it.
Then I wake,
a weekend dawn. The day
will wander through its plan,
a few hours' drive
to fetch my son for his night
at my home. I'm getting ready
to hear of his war,
the one someone prepares him

in a room without windows. I too
will figure to uproot my life
to save him from it. He won't know
until the war, the time,
is over. I won't tell him,
and he will have found
his way through with,
from me, nothing.

A Rabbit in the Soup is *Magnifique*

A rabbit in the soup is *magnifique*
unless it is alive—rampant,
superb, rags of spinach plastered across its feet
like flags on the heels of Victory,
hopping mad, repudiating
explanation, eyes black with hatred.
What we committed will never leave us,
the impulse of regret, far from ameliorating
winds us down into an extra tiny dimension
in which we circle endlessly like a carrot-leaf
in a drainpipe too small for oblivion.
After a while the rabbit never ceasing to fume
freezes gradually into statuary
and before we rise to leave which we now can do
we break off one forepaw as a passkey
for a door we can expect. Going out of that place
is like rising into sky, a dark one
of curds and spiderwebs
with the outrage fading in our ears
growing more neutral echoing from these marble walls
on either side where we begin to make out diagrams
nearly indiscernible from the veins of stone but labeled
in an almost legible script. Too much here to know.
Soon we will stoop and pick up compasses and small lights
as if for a cave maze, though still we are rising,

coming out into such light that only two or three things
can be seen at all—a lintel,
a brass bowl of flower petals,
and hanging down to a floor we can only feel
from a height we hardly guess, a bell-rope
with a loop knotted at the height of hands.
This is the time to ask how many we are,
two, three, or a cloud as of electrons,
generations, conference around the rope,
a people, a pair. One hand reaches to pull
and the sky splits just as you would foresee
raining all around a crowd of melting brown sweet gobbets
with eyes of red stone. Then come the glasses,
hornrim and wire, some with elastics, bifocal, dark.   ·
Then it's the heads of dolls, then shoes. Then falls
the sound of glass breaking for years, a continuous
shush. Then suddenly it is morning,
and they are taking away all the Jews.

A SIDESTREET IN CHANIA

Things not in the box are lost. Some may be found, a few. Introduced among
and to the things already in the box, something becomes something else.
Inkstone. Glyph.

How did anything get inside the box? I don't know, I've seen it happen. Until
the first thing was brought into the box, there was no box. That's the right
size to fit but the wrong color.

The world contracts into the box. It is happy to fit. Between partitions, ev-
erything from the world invents its place.

This bluejay feather frayed at the distal end.

I wanted to put in that attractively yellowed photograph of my grandfather
on my father's side. Though I can try to put things into the box, and fail, and

things can try to enter the box, and fail, I can't prevent things from getting into the box. A feather is one thing, a beak is another. Not the beak.

A body washed up yesterday outside the city in a widow's dress. A farm girl on her way to school found it and set her satchel carefully on the sand. She fretted that her assignments might be lost.

The box presumes what a *thing* is. What a thing *is* is nothing until it enters into the box. What segment of that courtyard. What chip. Inkstone of my heart. Of my hand, glyph.

Hmong weaving, six by seven centimeters.

The stitches, yellow and brown and blue, in the buff cloth, point up the feather's barbules' interlocking hooklets. Its calamus in turn, translucent, holds the thin weave out to the sunlight, or would if it weren't for the containing box, though the box is why it happens.

Through accident, a German's yacht crushes a fishing boat against the stone pier. Among the flinders bob some bearing the boat's saint's name.

While the box is a place where nothing appears to happen, because things appear they happen, as far as I can see, with my waning eyes in which the world dwindles. If it were possible to speak of opening and closing the box, it would be easier to count.

This shard of earth, or part of a shard, slippery clay once but gone heartwood-hard in a kiln shaken to the ground before Homer breathed.

In the company of the feather, the weaving and the earth regard each other in the kinship of hands, though hands long dead. In the company of the weaving, feather and earth, the weight and the light, remember the vocation of carrying what they used to belong to.

The box takes a shine to eternity. Doesn't traffic in stuff or crud, purely formal, like spats. Has it a hasp? It needs no clasp. It harbors a thin smell, soot and ledgers. Neither inkstone nor accident. A wing's no thing. What part of me could think to fit?

A boy who couldn't read or hear has burned a cat in a bag on the harbor wall.

Now that the earth is here, the feather calls the weaving brown and yellow and the weaving comes to admire the sturdy shaft, the rachis that divides and supports the spread vane. The feather muses and the weaving dreams. The earth grows old, glyph of itself, aglow. The weaving softens, agog with subtle gathers. Ever the feather intricates.

Book of matches from a defunct taverna.

Windborne across the Libyan Sea, Saharan dust pools in the bowls of spoons.

T S A

In the terminal, where madnesses
converge to make the path
bent and the way strait and the bag
pass the mechanical magnificent
nose the size of an S U V
I watched the man

open one it didn't like
—the old lady stood looking
beyond security's black ribbon
while he depacked and rummaged—
and having found the bad thing,
a slender bottle of café-au-lait liqueur

that he swabbed for residues then slid again
into the wool stocking enlisted for its protection,
gather with latex hands the stray
folds of the underwear,
the shapeless robes and snow-white slippers,
and pat them back in place.

To Carry Water in the Hands

I
to the face
to splash awake
to sip

II
to the wounded man, hunched
in the corner of a broken wall.
"Jesus" he repeats
like a woman in ecstasy
or labor. We cry
"Medic!" two or three times and run
to the stream to bring him what we can,
the canteen vanished somewhere down the hill,
we scoop some of the broth of earth
into our hands and hold them
together as well
as we can, rising, jogging back up the trail
whose dust settles a little on the tiny pool of it
before we reach him. He'll take it in
as best he can
and lean his head back
against the wall, silent a moment,
not satisfied
but assuaged, the eagerness
we lose last.

III
across the room.
Out of the dell, across the field,
over the wall to the road, along the road
toward town; under the first gate into the square,
past the empty fountain within the last precinct,
beneath the arch; up the stairs,
down the hall

to the door and through it,
across the room.
Here.

IV

In trying to carry
water in the hands
the thumbs
stick out like deaf antennae
or stupid phallic decorations
on a tree as serious as any tree
cut down can be. We don't have
to think about it, pressing
together the abductor digiti
minimi of left hand and right hand,
folding one sheaf of fingers
flat against the other—we have
a word for it, *cupped*,
we have always known it,
we take it in our hands and run.

V

is doomed
by agitation, gravity,
the capillary seam between padded bones,
despair. It drips,
sloshes and runs out.
Held still it holds a while, a pool
shimmering at its edge,
magnifying the grottoes of the palms,
catching the light and throwing it
in our eyes, entranced
by the gravity and agitation of this world
its ecstasy of labor
that nothing needs to help.

VI

from the meniscus of the stone-walled spring
rising from the vein of earth
simply to the mouth, a brief lively journey
up through air
just faster than it seeks ground again—
we have done this over and over
before we invented pots,
glasses and flasks, buckets, flagons and butts

and still, when the quest
for a vessel, in the cupboard
in another room down the hall
behind the tureen and the cheesegrater,
feels, somewhere below thinking, like too much, we place
the two hands together in the ancient way
to dip up the clarity we need to replenish
and lift it to lips
we hardly heard tell us they were dry.

REVIEW

The late images on bread
(halftone emulsion baked in,
developed by slow toasting
under a broiler) all four

have a special gravity
and ease: the third most haunting,
portrait of a man in the brown
overcoat and felt hat

of the forties, on a bench,
forearms angled in
across his knees. We feel for him
to fail as a father would

waste metaphysics. In the end
most intimate of virtues
I have never known
art-work smell so good.

THE WORLD SHOWER CURTAIN™

Except for the green,
salmon, custard and putty continents,
the world is clear,
the water of the world,
and through it shines
not the woman in the bath
antarctic in a bed of steam
but the woman in the shower, nearer
nipple pointing out Reykjavik,
pubis throwing wide
the Pillars of Hercules.

Reflected from skin,
drops cling to the inner
surface and blur the lines
the scrim of desire
hangs on, as the curtain hangs
from silver sky-hooks
and shivers at her lifted arms
as though tectonic magma roiled it.

The eye strives through brume,
each bead the lens
of a new projection, not
Mercator's monstrous north and south,
topheavy Greenland and fat Australia,
something more Equal Area, closer
to true, if truth
were visible. I always knew

there was a woman behind the world,
who furls it, shrugs aside
her cloak of water and stands forth
combing and contemplating
her silver fall of mirror.

READER, WRITER

When we go down into sleep
we keep the whole
breath thing going,
the heart-and-kidneys kit,
and even, when a voice says
Turn over, turn. We don't lose
balance on the narrow bed.
As if almost nothing were missing.
In the light, we rise knowing
within a few pages
our place in the manuscript.

MAUD DE CHAWORTH

Dear Charles. I write
from a cold place;
colder than Wales.
You have not yet
been here I think.
My third daughter
Eleanor had
a daughter Joan
et cetera,
and nineteen or
twenty acts of
generation
on, there you were

or there, if you
insist, you are.
Between the names
you recognize
from family
gossip and graves—
the coterie
who built your world
by living it—
and craggy names
you see in books
of this icy
upland the past,
is a vast crowd
of strangers, who
mill about with
not quite, from a
certain point of
view, yours more than
mine, no purpose.
I believe you
know Eleanor,
in a manner
of speaking, from
the poem about
the tomb where she
and her husband
are carved—second
husband Richard
the Arundel,
not sweet young John—
the rhyme that says
that what remains
of us is love,
or what we love's
remains, or some
words of that kind,

or not unkind,
refusing and
wanting to say.
People try so
hard, and for so
compressed a time.
I fretted nights
over my eight
young—and it's true,
all of them died—
but meanwhile Maud
my namesake had
her spring husband
de Burgh and then
de Ufford her
autumn; and my
Henry's little
Blanche, the wild and
frail, finally
did well enough
with the Gaunt man,
aside from his
Catherine, whose
sister married
young Geoff Chaucer—
when the plague killed
Blanche he wrote that
other nice poem
about the Duchess;
and their Henry
and then the next
followed and they
are history
you may have read.
Cold. There are few
animals here—
Laika, Washoe,

Hodge, Clever Hans—
in this human-
built nonplace like
your Internet,
brisk, burgeoning,
untrustworthy;
a kind of zoo
to look at such
specimens of
what was as me.
You put us here
remembering.
You have other
living to touch,
talk with, make tea
and music with.
Looking back out
against the wind
makes the eyes tear;
we all do it.
We are data
pullulating
until you send
across the waste
from time to time
your remnant love.
I do not write
you now for some
novel reason—
death-defying,
beyond-the-grave
dire mission, find
my forgotten
will, rescue the
cat trapped behind
the disused stove;
I write because

there's nothing more
to be done here
and because you
asked so nicely.
As ever, Maud.

SYMPOSION

for Steve Diamant

—and so descry a plot
like a meal in a Greek restaurant
our compatriot the archaeologist

is in charge of ordering.
It must begin with wine and with wine go on
and end, except

for the coda of his trenchant,
ritually wetted, candle-sealed cigar.
Earlier it has occurred to me

in the chasm between bites or the long slide
from *tarámosalata* to *tirokafterí*,
that it would be impossible to love

a group of humans more. Bring not
at last the *baklavá* lest in the black
midden of sugar-blood behind the eyes

love choke and stifle.
Sober in the prodigal midst,
we dream of an end

in *raki*, what
best becomes the grape
when all the wine's pressed out of it:

the twice distilled, from
(drop by drop)
the Arabic for *sweat*.

And look, we have passed on
from the toys of time. Behold
the wreckage of the table.

THE LENS

In the old quarter, daylight rhymes with dust.
The shop's shaped like a wick with flame inside.
We bring him time, in pieces, to adjust.

A finger's lettered every pane, like lust
Or justice. Air is what light lies behind
In the old quarter; daylight rhymes with dust.

Our story: children of displaced mistrust,
With jumbled bags we came, with hearts disrhymed.
We brought crushed time in pieces to adjust.

Winter. Over the cordillera gust
Sands fine as lampblack. Mind, or do not mind,
In the old quarter, daylight rimed with dust.

Slat-glimpsed, those arc-blue workbench sparks, discussed
Into the nights, like mortgage, leave us tired.
We take our time, in pieces, to adjust.

Blind as a god he gathers what he must
Give out again. Roses are growing wild
In the old quarter. Daylight rhymes with dust
We bring him. Time is pieces to adjust.

Song Without Words

I. Measure

unit			
second	1588	\<French\>	as time; in geometry 1391 (Chaucer)
minute	1377	\<French\>	
hour	1250	\<French\>	as 1/12 of daytime; as 1/24 of day, 1330
day	950	\<Teut.\>	originally time of daylight
week	900	\<Teut.\>	
month	888	\<Teut.\>	
year	960	\<O. Eng.\>	
decade	1605	\<Latin\>	as time; as ten of anything 1594
century	1626	\<Latin\>	as time; as 100 of anything 1533
millennium	1711	\<Latin\>	
aeon	1933	\<Latin\>	as time unit; as whole age of universe 1647

II. Sequence

	date		
month	888	\<Teut.\>	
week	900	\<Teut.\>	
day	950	\<Teut.\>	originally time of daylight
year	960	\<O. Eng.\>	
hour	1250	\<French\>	as 1/12 of daytime; as 1/24 of day, 1330
minute	1377	\<French\>	
second	1588	\<French\>	as time; in geometry 1391 (Chaucer)
decade	1605	\<Latin\>	as time; as ten of anything 1594
century	1626	\<Latin\>	as time; as 100 of anything 1533
millennium	1711	\<Latin\>	
aeon	1933	\<Latin\>	as time unit; as whole age of universe 1647

You Could Look It Up

Google the final lines your lover sang
on the way out; and what the Sort-bird said;
ideal dimensions for a boomerang;
tips for the feeding of the careless dead . . .
Back to those last, melodious words: they rang
a dim bell in the aisle-seat overhead.
You've read them carved in ice or spelled in leaves,
a source no query you devise retrieves.

The world is muddled to the muddle-headed.
To the alert mind all is plain as paint.
Things come with user manuals embedded.
Windows open and close without complaint.
Only the bad or careless get beheaded.
No lover needs to wonder *Is you ain't*
my baby since we all say all we mean.
No untoward slips, ever, in between.

In the age of information, any child
with basic keyboard skills can know its father.
Itself's another matter—morphed, misfiled—
password-proscribed—we wonder if you'd rather
rest from your questing? Here, we have compiled
the table of your dreams. No need to bother
the drowsy kennelsful. What you can know,
or anyone, is here. Enjoy the show.

For Mr Quidnunc Pressed Upon the Wheel

For Mr Quidnunc, pressed upon the wheel,
no meal is adequate, no shock too short,
no cat too comfy. Nothing in excess
is not his motto, though he thinks it is
and writes his nephew weekly to say so.
He thinks that he is pressed upon the wheel

and he is pressed, not on the wheel he thinks
but one of gentler curvature, which is
to say, bigger. It might eclipse the moon,
a turning for this ache of its own sake,
croquet's excruciating afternoon . . .
(This early in the game we're free to make

any legal move, when plot has not
got wind of us yet.) Mr Quidnunc knows
less than he thinks and more than he lets on;
the better of him is rarely to be had.
His bedside table snugly holds, of all
imaginable controls, the most remote.

      Once something gave him pause. It had a shape
      like rain on rusted iron. It had a name
      like *Santa Claus* or *Yggdrasil*, emitted
      a smell like punishment. It made a sound
      no louder than the wheel on its oiled hub.
      The more he blinked the more it was still there,

      as an alley, followed, follows in the dark.
      He stood his quaky ground thinking to stare
      it down. (Usually we pause a moment
      here. As the fingers of the highest tide
      touch, with apparent shyness that is too
      implacably false to be called coy, a bottle

      lodged at the ultimate spring line, and draw
      around it, under, lift and tumble it
      away toward Zanzibar; as if we were
      the empty bottle, capped for travel, tranced,
      containing neither message nor prescription,
      wave's, wind's and current's temporary toy,

we pass onward.) He has never stared it down.
He finds himself at ends of working days

amazed at his back yard. Over the bushes
a butterfly can undecide for hours.
He listens to the mockingbird with care.
One beetle with another end-to-end

drags her the length of Mr Quidnunc's deck.
The iridescent grackles stride his grass
flinging over their shoulders the gift-wrap leaves.
The locust on the locust sings and saws.
An osprey drops a feather at his feet
from somewhere near the axle. A new old man,

he is overcome and overcome for good,
so lightened that he throws himself with ease
into the trees or the wise air, illiterate
with happiness, with no idea why
a man should sleep all night. He sleeps all night
(though Mr Quidnunc's nephew's tossed and turned).

TOO FAR—HE SAID

for George Psychoundakis

Too far—he said—and this tin can
will rattle to scrap. The path is good
for goats but the right rear wheel loathes it.
I came here every summer as a boy
with my father, give his soul peace
now that his body has it, to carry firewood
down to the winter house, but not on wheels.
Those faggots jabbed the leather pad on my back,
every step when they rubbed together they sang like crickets
in the panic of autumn. Pass me that bugle,
I need to hail the lonely ghost of Kyría Elpída—
the house is through those thorns. Ask me about her
when I'm drunk. That son of a whore
tire wants to blow like a dead seal.
My father if he heard a pup crying at night

he'd pull on his trousers, go find the yard
and sit with it an hour or till daylight,
but he drove his brother clean out of business.
Up there, that cliff the sun's picked out
with the fort wall up top like a drop of honey,
a bastard of a low cave creeps in and in,
the soldiers used it. It stinks of sheep
most of the year. The flesh has its uses,
they used to say, and some of them make sense.
When my bones shake like this thing
they can shovel me into that patch there,
under the olive terrace, where water runs
after a big rain and the next day,
the very next, flowers by the yellow million.
I will now say—he said—what I like:
I like the way the light changes over the bay
too slowly for a movie camera, nearly too fast
to see, any time you look up it's new again
dawn to dark. Up here too, but the wind
flowing down the mountain has greater influence,
turning leaves over and over. Anywhere
no shortage of vagaries. Well
our hands teach us attention and our bowels patience
—if you don't think out the door is an adventure
you never had this clutch—but nobody learns
how to live a thousand years and like it.
There—he said—I said it would go,
flat as an old scrotum. There is another.
When my uncle's house undercut in a flash flood
we used a jack like this, bigger, to raise the corner
till she stood straight or nearly, like my aunt,
and shoved rocks under, a mouthful of rocks.
After, we should have shored with baulks
but the jack stayed for seven years.
One day another deluge took the proximal side
and the whole house fell in a bone-heap
so my aunt tipped off the sill and broke the other leg.

She went home to her village, so my uncle died.
This tree has watched that valley since the Plagues.
From the hill over the bay you see waves break
and the sound of them flows up so that you hear one
while you see the next—you'd never know
if you didn't climb up and down—because sound
must wander up through the grass and thistles.
Aristotle explained that noumena praise phenomena
and stones teach us, he said, by seeking earth.
Now we will go on. Here is the rule
of pistachios, you eat till the hand
is full of shells. Later that season
we decamped to the sea and became its citizens.
By the bay my fourteenth name-day,
my mother's thirty-fifth and last, the day
after the spider-sack of the white sky split and spilled
Germans, or like milkweed, or spicules in the eye.
Yesterday into my nephew's place wandered a German
couple, two children squeezed from a pastry nozzle.
Enough. That hill resembling a closed fist, knuckles down
on the tabletop, by the wrist a spring flows
for two villages, so they used to fight.
Nobody fires a pistol into the rafters any more
at weddings. Even the priest did, late.
I think—he said—I am getting old, though
I don't think I smell like an old man yet.
Those girls in the variety store. In Cairo once on leave
I saw the Zoo, even though diminished
they said by shortages from submarines,
and the earth dumbfounded me again for strangeness,
like a traveling peddlar with his wonder bag.
Hand me that what do you call him cellular,
I will arrange dinner. No. What good is what
can talk if not over mountains,
like the megaphone trucks selling trees and fish
slow-trawling down the village street.
My father built a proper shop, bought from the boats,

sold to the mothers every morning. This finger-end
I lost to learning to clean them. I love the hour
of evening, cats on patrol, swallows diving mad
—preposterous expenditures, and after giving up
one ovary and the bones' cores, but who wouldn't envy them—
and the headland going gold then iron then lapis,
before they made one in town that was our cinema.
Polaris stood still over the one peak, or nearly,
we never saw them both at the same time. Look over,
the young olive within an inch of her precipice,
the field sloping below like a laced bodice. Now the right
front complains like a pack of jack-dogs
and there is no other, the creator has given up
on this machine, who knows it. It was my father's
mother's cousin the Turks took after a raid,
they cut his head off and shoved a stick in it,
then wedged it upright and practiced marksmanship
from ten yards, for an hour, so there was nothing
much to gather and bury with the rest. I'll tell you though
—he said—we hardly ever killed a German
anywhere near the homes we yearned most to cleanse
since whoever did they burned his village
down to the stones and shot the family.
Enough. That bird is *karakaxa*,
the one saying his name again and again, a thief
and clever as a pig at it. Smell here. A mocker
dances without a tambourine. I commend that goat
contemplating beneath the low vault of his horns
his shadow and the shadow of his beard. A good day, and
a good thing. Pouring honey in the dark
is a waste of joy. And there—
I knew it would. From here we go on foot.

from THE PIGFOOT REBELLION

LYING AWAKE 8/24/72

around my ears the sounds rise in slow eddies
high in the center pulse the ridged whistles of crickets
the swish of a few cars lifts midnight blue to the window
now and then your pages rustle to my right
so I think of a goatherd sitting on warm stone
rhythmically brushing his goatskin musette on the stone
the goats are amused but browse and leave his gazing
cicadas above sway chewing the air in the high branches
beside his stone a stream whispers of oceans
so far away there is time for a long sleep down the hills
past stones and goatherds and on through cities
past windows where the whispers rise like blue mists
to mingle with the brushing of page on page till the lady
sleeps and the white sea takes the stream

A LITTLE SONG

She beyond all others in deepest dreams comes
back. You shun sleep, lying in darkness, breath held,
hearing that voice over the rustling dry grass
    breathing in darkness.

Walk for miles each day, with a dog to watch, pen
paper, ink, try, focus attention somewhere
else. But Mi, Sol, Re go the notes her voice slips
    into your blind heart.

Once you knew each inch of her body. No more.
Only one thing, caught in your faithful ear, still
lives. Your eyes lie. Even in dreams the face fades.
    Only a singing.

She's your cane these days. When you tap, she tells how
far you've strayed. Tap trees by the road, you hear how

hollow things are. Listen. You'll hear in high limbs
   voices of dry leaves.

To Shadow

Noon sets the tips of pines on fire;
trunks' shapes are half-guessed. The goshawk's
claws glint among ragged feathers.
My feet trace out the hurried way.

When the field and its winding path
answer no question, pose nothing,
my stride slows; easy light casts down
the tree behind me till, a shade,
I wind through the branching shadow.
Evening's levelling everything.

When I see the hawk's smooth winging
home, it seems the world lays down arms
forever. (Hunched in the thick grass,
a blind spot swimming in this blind
repose, a mole thrusts through its long
labor, through this short peace of night.)

Light wears thin. I hear doves whistling
in the dark. On the wide field, day
lies down to sleep, a man worn dark,
his own shadow's weary hunter.

Before My Father Before Me

My mother's mother painted her
Perhaps in 1936
At perhaps thirteen
In the tentative light of a White Mountain dream.

The house not shown
Is sold to strangers now.
It might be raked leaves the color of her hair
She watches, flushed.

Her high silk blouse is the same
Blue-green as the mountains,
A color almost of sea.
In 1936 her eyes,
Half as old as when I met them, half
As old as I am now,
Were dry as leaves,
Bright as the scattered leaves.

My grandmother nearly always painted trees.
In this there are only mountains, things
Keeping their blue distance.

The old lady is dead. Her brush
Made these mountains of a half-known mother's wish
Or set them down as they were by her daughter's eyes
Composed of vague desire and the sea.

She dreams of distance
Hazy and wide as the North Atlantic,
Peopled with strangers;
Holds it still as she holds her blazing
Head for her mother's brush.
Between pale lips she
Breathes the world that invests her
Into being,
Formless,
Perfect:
A woman with my own face,
Thinking of other things.

from TRUE NORTH

Whatever branch you dreamed
It sprouted leaves, bore fruit,
Gardened itself, redeemed
The old dispute

In a dream. You woke and found
The garden all deranged—
But everything around
A little changed.

WAKING UP

There are miles of this: and every storefront
concept of the land of the dead gives back—
now that the sun's dropped low in your eyes—
your face, as if in a badly hung painting
you leave without ever having really seen.
What was ever there? The contamination
of living not by dying but by death, galling
as Socrates; the fetishes of yew and cryogenics
and the long agenda of despair; the locked
glass doors, opaque, that like a cop you try
one after another down a row whose end,
invisible, is only the beginning of another
beat—in the breath of dreams like this you smell
something clean and inescapable, jolting
as skunk on an old road at midnight,
something to recall those colloquies with the moon
you held an hour ago, before it set, something
so pure with purpose it doesn't matter what
the purpose is, to me, if it's all the same to you.

CATCHING A RAY

I

Where the gray beast of the water
cornered itself into harbor,
that mouth amid whiteness
gasped on the raw deck
a secret thrust from beneath
the brittle hide of the sea

                        —This

surfaces again as I lurch
awake speechless and wet
in the gray dawn, caught
in the webbed sheets:

                              the ordinary
lead scales of the flounder
spilled out of the net
around my landsman's shoes;
that lividness spilled out
shocking among them; and how
nothing speaks but the air
is full of petitions, laments
a routine catastrophe, grinding
of gears gone wrong
down in the waves' heavy
housing. It wasn't this
I came out here to see.

        II

Suddenly no one wants to be
where he is. We are all
(the fisherman and I, the ray,
these dumb flustered flounder)
embarrassed, some of us ready
to die of embarrassment;
none of us prepared for the moment
to say what might have been
said to correct a day gone bad,
writhing on the dark boards.
We who can breathe breathe
in the shallows of the sky,
gaping. This one on the deck—
eyeless, like a half-
remembered face, refusing
to finish itself
                    (whose flight
has been a kind of glimmering
supple vocabulary, the right
phrase even now caught on the tip
of a wing that flexes in a last
eloquence, the mouth trying

in silence as a throat tries
to croak waking words
to tell what has been
dreamed)
      —in the end
leaves in the undiluted air
a leather corpse and, when I turn
my eyes away, an image
seared against the sky.

III

Are these things meant to come
lurching out of the nowhere
that is the sea, to break
the surface tension guarding
world from world, to bring
everything right out on deck
where the gunnels, which saved us
from the sea, have locked us in
to look at it, just as it is?
You say, *Why should I carry
such a thing around?*

Lying back, you know
the possible corrections:
to throw the witness back
into the sea, or yourself,
to sink back into sleep,
saying, *It's early yet.*

Somehow the white belly,
the black boards of the deck
and gunnels, the seaweed-green
slick boots of the fisherman,
and even the slowly silvering
scales of dying flounder
catching an unpromised fire

between the gray dawns
of sky and the closed sea:
these colors fasten me
where I am; and the deck that bears
everything it can bear
rides a little closer to the waves.

Things to Attend To

It didn't have to be that way at all.
If there had been lions, you would
Deal with lions, you'd learn the heat,
The cold, Urdu, Hopi, the proper treatment of the dead, the formulas
For greeting a second cousin or a path you'd left,
How to save subway tokens, the name for the back of your head,
Your name. Instead you stand with your arms folded in the sunlight,
Almost aware of cotton that hovers under your right fingers
And the minute resistance of the grass against your soles, watching
The young black locust, thinking, In a few months it will smell
Sweeter than remembered rain. Elsewhere, the women are weeping
At the War Memorial, the men are weeping, the children
Are standing guard duty with grand strides. Something in your stance
Resembles the bushman waiting for a certain elephant
That will feed his family for months. Casual as you are,
Lounging like a pimp in Marseilles, you recall the children
Gripping their old weapons for the sake of memory, a memory
They almost have, like the thought of a place you almost visited, a smell
You couldn't place the first time you smelled it, though it's always seemed
Familiar as anything, as though it had happened to somebody you almost
Were. A grasshopper springs at the locust trunk and misses,
Shoving the tree into sudden shape, big as a monument,
Too big to be seen, almost. And you think, What is the name
For the locust that would include it? Surely the bushman's name
Includes the smell of the elephant after it's dead, and the smell
Of the man who represents the elephant in the dance afterwards—
There could have been no end to it. The grasshopper

Gives up and lies down in the dirt for seven years.
Never quite knowing why—you'll wonder
When it's too wet to go slogging here through raw grass—
You decide to move, and you move. Your name will include it.
If your hands slip into your pockets, it's because
You don't know what else to do with them.
Your name will include it.
The locust waves, but it's not goodbye.

ON MY MOTHER'S BIRTHDAY

It's easy to remember
my father said: Bastille
Day, but instead
November. This
Bastille Day you were still
around for another
pair of weeks.
The end of July was my
father's birthday,
the next day, mine;
the following day
you died.
          You did. You
turned away into
your ghost
going off in your last daze:
on a face drawn
from my mother's, all
your old expressions
fixed in place
by the drugs for pain, exposed
to our quick eyes.
You didn't want much
to go outside, falling
forward step by step

on the nurse's arm,
to sit in the sun
that warmed the long cushion.
We shivered a little
in your skeptical shade.

Once I forgot,
writing a set of songs
for someone else for Christmas.
Then you were a file of ashes
in a cabinet, and then
diluted in the ocean. Nothing. Now
Christmas comes
around as usual;
my father plans to visit;
one holiday pursues
the last into the next
inexorable year.
                    There isn't much
to say to a distributed
sample of chemicals, rerouted
into the lives of plankton.
I have no say.
But sixty years ago
today, your entry made
a tiny change in things;
and when I take on
the universe—
when the stars clash
over my rages, petrels fly
to my own north,
and the salt sings—
your going shifts
the galaxies
disasterward, and all
the horses in their fields
kneel down in terror.

DOMESTIC

That nest hands empty now
we thought of as ours
in pride because it occupied

our dogwood, and the three
eggs that the sun glanced
nearly white and two

fat robins trading places
on them and later hastily
relaying crop after crop up

of worm to the three wide yellow
beaks that gradually grew
heads and wings and all, all

were ours like children, more
than tripling the places around our table.
Bright black eye, white-ringed,

through dogwood. Now the rain's
beginning finishes dispersing
the long collection, down,

vines, twigs, twine, wild
candy wrappers, excelsior, the sky
taking apart the day we missed

dinner because we couldn't miss
the third one beating its panic way
out of the dismantling

nest, branch to branch to
join its place in the singing
ring, the loose cached ring

around our yard, the ring of harsh,
defining, catcall drunken cries
kept up all night. Then gone.

Over a Cup of Tea

Sometimes when the evening gathers most attentively about itself,
like a cape full of inside pockets, any machine with clean lines,
I have wished for a life of wisdom, the kind the old men

carve into walnut shell in the marketplaces
of holy cities. I think of Ludolf van Ceulen in 1610, the German
dying in Leyden at the city's height still roiling with scholars,

Scaliger and the rest; composing for his tombstone, graven deep
as a voice shaken firm by love, the figures of his life:
thirty-five places of pi;

giving both upper and lower limit to intimate—*siste viator*—
the work remaining after his years of calculation
"*multo labore*" picking his way from error of defect to error

(as the mathematicians used to say) of excess, toward an end
only his own.
When I sit beside you in the unraveling light, when my knowledge

of your face can most astound me, I understand
that between too little and too much lay something worth
pursuing, some *ratio*, a squaring of circles, some place

where one is happy never to arrive.
The evening is like that, working its way toward night
which is not a place but a station, like Leyden on the way

to Haarlem from Brussels or the east, where nothing has stopped
for centuries; yet saying all the time, so quietly,
This is an end of everything.

Reckoning up the day and the coming night, you and I strike our balance
for a moment, over a cup of tea. Having made
errors of all kinds, we have learned one another

approximately. We feel our way between two mysteries
into a third. Night rises, and with a common motion we gather in
each other, all we can hold.

LEBENSRAUM

Mistranslations from the Southern Sung,
The movies, late Impressionism, *Vogue*—
All versions of the natural strew the mind's
Contemporary Classic living room.
Off in the corner hunkers something wild,
An Art Nouveau TV, first model year,
Glassed like the porthole of a sunken ship.

Out of the murk swam something cute that sang
Of other worlds, location a bit vague.
To see, like Satan, Earth behind the moon's
Looming—a vulnerable star—could rhyme
The loony tune of what was with what would,
The long deplored appointments of your yore,
Heaven, and other stock from the same shop.

What we want's boulder, rock, stone, gravel, sand,
The tiny truth, and none of your damned Wag-
nerian mythy hooch. The earth reminds
Its grand children of something that was Rome.
The last by God green-flowered man was Wilde.
They dance divinely, past the air. The Year
Two Thousand learns, gobbet by gobbet, shape.

For Zachary

After the one swung limb and scramble, all
     the rest of up eases. Deciduous
          stair, ramifying opportunity
and all, the goal's not getting above, but
     into thick matrix balanced on the one
          peg leg, sturdy stilt, sap pipe for the green
crown of shield-shaped sugar-factory offspring
     one distance calls *leaves* and one calls *the tree.*
          Rest in a crotch, just as the genes intend.
Here is heaven, home, shelter heartwood-sure
     till the next development; relevant
          neither to brain nor penis; elephant-
steady, cicada-loud, starlinged, boardwalk
     of the many-legged. Though dinner's down,
          the heart is full up, flush, at liberty.
Zacchaeus climbed his tree to find his Lord.

The Difference Engine

A freeway, a double stroke
of fingers idling down
the flank of the continent
from New Brunswick by Fredericton to Florida
halfway to Miami, an expressive definition
of the skin of the land
touching major ganglia,
Boston, New York, et cetera,
Philadelphia, Washington. Ninety-Five,
a password by which we aim each other
to each other's wakes, parties, rallies,
by which name in our rambling mouths
all Providence might recognize
Savannah as from just
down the road, the way a tree

continues the ground I stand on
up to a vireo ready to get up
and fly south. And Ninety,
a memory bringing Seattle to Boston
associating at Chicago with Eighty's dream
of San Francisco, Youngstown, Omaha, makes its own
connections. Eisenhower,
thinking only to get the troops
there in a big hurry, laid down
the neural reticulation of the nation
that in a science-fiction movie or Plato
could lift away from the ground
to live independently among the stars
feeding on their photonic fire
and reveling among strange terrors.
From a thousand miles up the Great Wall
curls like a noodle of DNA—
singular according to our scale.
This morning I woke up cold and happy,
the sky the pale color of a teacup,
and I remembered that if I put on
enough shirts I could stand in the brown yard
and think about the warmth of my wife's body
still under the blanket, if I wanted
I could get in the car and drive north,
if I said I was thirty-five years old
it would be true until next year and for all
I can recall the last time
I woke up happy it was
today, as if
days were like Tolstoy's families, only
the sad ones individual.
This is morning like a bank account
in a new town, or a chess problem, all
incipience, when it's possible to think
not of deforming the world it is but moving
through it—no,

within it, not light through greased paper or
neutrinos through a world of lead
but from place to place making
a difference, destroying
nothing. My toes wriggle in old boots.
The tree-eater down the hill hums
its C below middle C with occasional
rising arias and the man
with the power blower strapped to his back
strides the street keeping the leaves
moving. Suddenly I recognize the tune
in my head as Ella singing "'Tis
Autumn" but under it running something
bebop, "Confirmation," an airbrush painting
of cirrus or a light rime on grass. Icing.
Overhead whole carpets of small birds
flicker through figures too quick almost
for the eye: of the maps of catastrophe
theory or of warped spacetime or the deft grandeur
of high bridges, the Jamestown at Newport,
the Tappan Zee, the Mercer Island over Lake Washington
or most, maybe, the one proposed
over Gibraltar,
out of this world. You know
their heading as well as I, those tiny
singers of *me, me*, as the pointer poised
on the gas company calendar knows it, the page headed
NOVEMBER and every seventh day
red like a seventh wave breaking
over the shelf of the town. In half an hour
the sun will clear itself
from the last of the scrub pine
and a big bell toll somewhere to mean
Go to work. But I've been at work
for hours: indexing my life in a night's dreams,
translating myself to a new world, waking,
leaving one place always and coming into another

to think about it, not just whistling
back to the birds but mouthing *hearth*,
soil, what the weathered Saxons called
the sky, *welkin*. The ground
breathes up into the new day and its breath
shows in thin wisps, and mine. The words lift up
out of the life and make shapes on bare air
like telegrams, deeds, Alcaics,
likenesses we live by
means of, like the view
down the backyard slope, how
cars named for gods and animals fill the wide
blue air, in which they glitter, with what they burn;
as when the plants remade the planet's
sky for themselves—and for us, it turned out.
The house is full of books full of them, shelves
full of the books—answers
to the riddle, What solid object
is all inside? where *solid* means
indivisible except by violence.
We could drive east
away from them all, to find
after the ever sparser farmhouses
and the ritardando of brush
the sea, so busy in detail, so
patient at large. When the man across the street
opens his door to the morning I start
to move around, kicking a little
at the clumped turf to seem intent. He calls
and waves and I raise a hand. His daily news
retrieved, he retreats. I go
like business to the side door of the garage
and open its odor of cold oil.
I let go the handle and step in and stand.
It's dark and abstract, a space of objects,
rags and cans, a tire framed by studs
on one somber wall, a box of magazines,

lawnmower. My hand on the car's roof
like reassuring a horse's rump,
I unlatch the driver's door and settle
down in the seat: Sixty-six! Dear dead road,
a few limbs still unburied through Oklahoma
and Arizona, stopped cold at California, living on
in a lot of hearts, in deep-carved
pathways, uncountable nerves that still recall
the sweep through Gallup, fighting
high winds in thunder outside Amarillo,
how Needles stands in awe of the one Mojave.
With quiet hands I bless the steering wheel.
Do you see by now that I'm dreaming this
lying in prison at Joliet, wrapped
in skins in a lean-to near Kalispell, near Caribou,
stirring in satin in Baton Rouge, about to wake
up to my wife, my husband, my mother, my sergeant,
my nurse, my job, my pension, my seeing-eye dog?
I shiver,
I'm back outside
in the sunlight back
of the house where the house
is laced up with the shadows of bare branches,
where a little movement shows
my wife in a high window half visible,
washed by light. Suddenly I want
to shout and jump on the springs of my toes and I
do, and I do again. My breath writes
inviolable on the vellum air.
She comes up closer to the glass,
shimmers between reflected clouds
and opens her robe to the swelling sun.
For a whole minute she blazes there,
and then she's gone.
When I can again, I turn and take in
the town spread down the hill
by block by block, the accumulative consequence

of the mill at the bottom's
river, the continuation
up to us, the last term. In a while
she joins me on time
for the hooter to fill the landscape
up like a reservoir and the day to begin
officially: breakfast and kiss quick, hurry down
to the looms or a scarred desk or the hourly gate-check
or guiding small parties through
a factory born again into history. Or maybe
we count cash for the gas
lock up the house, and then?
And then? Our story can be
anything you like, will be true
sometime, doesn't matter now to you or even us
the way what's cooking does. But the bench
I built from an oak slab out back stays put
from which I watch unfolding step by step
a process that has no single name or, if it does, a name
so etiolated by abstract associations as to remain
essentially speechless. Or it would be just
the name of the town. When you wait
for something to take
place in the world—
for the car that made the ordinary
wrong turn down the valley and disappeared
behind the station to find the turnaround
and show up again—you always experience
at least one moment of incredulous impatience
before it does, and half the time it doesn't
happen at all because of some
alternative possibility
forgotten or ignored or
discounted as too unlikely. Think of it: Too far
away to appear, the substantial bodies of swans
develop into the day's brightness on a small lake
anywhere. History repeats

itself because there is
nothing else for it to repeat. Lobsters lie,
enormous hands awkwardly at rest
before their pinched faces, elbow to elbow.
Among them scrambles the cleanup horseshoe crab,
chitinous boxing glove of a water-breather
older even than his job. Around our eaves and trees
the concentration of birds resembles the concentration
of men around a building site
or an accident. The complexity
of living, which is called
metabolism, change, a making and breaking, answers
to a description requiring about fifteen
thousand simultaneous differential
equations. I dreamed this morning of reading
a longish poem in short lines which
bored me. The folly
of setting out blind on a new road nearly repeats
the folly of staying in one place forever.
Consider (gather *sidera*,
stars, into constellation) this
net that bags the continent: Conway, Pennsylvania,
between Freedom and Economy, on the Ohio
just after the Allegheny and Monongahela
combine to make it; Conway in the middle
of Florida, just a section of Orlando now;
Conway in the flat delta of Faulkner County,
Arkansas, the biggest of the lot with its couple of colleges
and acres of school buses; Conway, Missouri,
smallest of all,
on the crypto-Sixty-Six now Forty-Four;
Conway, New Hampshire, despite the tourists,
tucked among White Mountains, a lake and dark woods
they don't know; the Massachusetts Conway
that grows wild fantasy; Conways of North and South
Carolina, the little and the large,
near Virginia, near the Atlantic; Conway

72 CHARLES O. HARTMAN

Springs, Kansas, westernmost, maybe
twenty-five miles from Oklahoma and the same
from Wichita, off I-35 and even off U.S.
One-Sixty that winds from Truman's birth
to Flagstaff, taking in the Comanche
National Grassland in Colorado. Wound around
fingers we can't see, the cat's cradle
makes neighbors who will never give
each other a thought, certainly never
meet or perceive a palm among them. Lost.
What keeps us from being
hopelessly lost in all this room is a set of names
associated with the acts of iron,
variation as mapped as Minneapolis
though changing as the pole
wanders from year to year.
To get from anywhere to any
other: a watch, a compass,
a set of tables filled
with the numbers of all places and of their bearing
on one another. A certain kind of person
that some days I wake up and think I am
or should be keeps these in the trunk
along with the jumper cables, N A S A blanket,
flares and spare fuses and fluids, sand for the snow
and maps the county gives us. And the tables?
Arithmetic in which the hand
so errs the eye demonstrably
never repairs the last residuum:
Errata of Errata. Thus the man
a century ago, brooding on the much misnumbered world.
Babbage's first machine (before
the Analytic Engine, pewter computer unbuilt and perfect)
from a list of figures certainly derived
could by the meshed meticulous crepitation of small wheels
effect such multiple addition as to print
whatsoever ordered sequence the Admiralty or Royal

Society desired—the Method
of Differences, totals accumulating
backward through the web of sums
to the truth of where the sailors are. How obsolete
this faith in place. It's not so much
how time passes I think as how it
piles up, thicker and thicker the farther you go
in any direction. The farther
the deeper, in a relation precise but not
direct. That is why buildings rarely reinforced
by presence fall apart, fall down to the ground,
why days descend growing yellower every hour
and why we find ourselves
this afternoon
so down the hill. If we take a bench
municipally placed on the mill bank
the riffle of wind will push
the water another way from its current
bearing a few leaves from the far shore past
the tripods and tetrapods of old timbers
baulking the long stream to make us wonder
which way a single word of water
bends, though we get the drift.
Speeding on, speeding, we shorten toward the goal.
Astronomers say so and in front of us
pace hand in hand the couples squat with age
making the most of the last weather
the sun will offer
at this price. For the day to go on so
we join the procession, walk and get somewhere,
the red wall of the edifice
where cloth was built up strand by strand
looming in the late sun's
preoccupation, realizing we've gone
another light-day, sixteen
billion miles and a fraction, finding our two hands
my right, her left impossible

to resolve in the light that's only failing
from the point of view of those who think light likes
to keep on forever.
Last night the T V *told us of* maintenance-
free beauty. *Love, I thought, in a world that loves*
what's new, we do our best together
gathering grace for the way we're going.
When daylight starts
to sink back wholly into the ground
we kiss and snuggle on the wharf like teenagers,
our hands moving over each other's back and shoulders
in the rhythm of comfort and admiration. Her name
is the name of the first teacher who brought
mathematics home to you, round as an egg.
Mine is a mark on paper, ideogram for *caterpillar*.
In the monad of our meshed hands
like those swimming fetuses Yin and Yang
not Boötes but Pisces, lies the rebus for
mirror, the one that cannot be
imposed on the other—and inside that
five laced with five unique
designs of whorl and loop by which
your index might be known from any other,
including your other own. Like any pure
being it speaks its single name, "I AM."
The mind like the world though
teems. Entranced by words it delights in reading
the cursive Great Wall and the chromosomes,
the history of its own accomplishment, history of light:
feeling its way into a grand circulation, like
the great Capes, Cod and Hatteras, Fear and Romain, Canaveral
where the satellites begin, putting out into vastness
a little way, to look back.
A road runs along the ridge
above the town, the river.
From the side of it, in the excellent dark
we can behold more stars than we know

what to do with—one of those nights
when you have your hands
full and are glad.
We can't make out the Cup or Crow, the Great
or Little Bear, Orion with his penis of three suns,
Balance or Bull or Hercules or any heroine
or hero among the eighty-eight beasts
and half-immortals that neighbor us—not for too few
visible fragments but too
strewn a sky, thick with the bushels of light,
a zenith so bright the clear
simplicities are lost, no
star's name known without the numbers
of its home. In so much brilliance
the weaving body of our river
at the bottom of the sky
between the stones and needs of the town
wends among streetlights and neon signatures
and the black blocks of storehouses
and the mill: a course aglow. My wife,
a blood-warm shadow, takes
one of my hands and we talk fast about nothing.
Our toes and fingers urge us down the hill
out of the unconditional
to the last house, whose lights invite us
to turn in, to be at the beginning
of the story of the town, its once
upon a time, to wake somewhere
or somebody here tomorrow.

from GLASS ENCLOSURE

GLASS ENCLOSURE

Sky-
light
water
beaded a snow moustache
going under the haze sun say
morning! Know it anywhere. These hands
almost still
the fingers so wise about moving
like a son of a bitch
and fold up sweet.
Step outside
or look twice.
Say in the Bible
Thy hands have made me.
What, hey
what can go wrong?
Elvin got it
Ray got it, days
I got it double. Morning
come to terms, flex, reflex,
yellow light in block chords.
No snow abides
but an alligator kind of thing
down corner and down right side
a drop cut loose. The heat is on.

Where these palms have been
no wonder the fingers fly.
Baby I mean you. Only hard thing
remembering to
breathe sometime.
Fool with it!
Hang the note out there on the fool end and wind.
Sky full of big bluster
with half a brain. Full of fantasy.
Chimneys and roofs of Paris

work of my hands flesh
work of my hands grace

work in my hands music
mark on my hands grace

musk on my hands flesh
mask of my flesh music

The print's pushed just a little, so the white
of this chair rail has milk's abundant brown
to it: white through and through, as the trees' light
clouded by muslin in the next, last room
washes to dry saffron through the screen door
ahead, down the numinous hall whose hardware
(a black softened by thousands of thought[less]
caresses) punctuates the eleven steps
left between here and the outside. Fear.
Intention. Stories of sheer air. The frail
tenons snugged through the back stile of the near
door where the middle rail attaches. Rail
and stile, mortise. Crewel sunflower. Pix.
Uninhabited noon. The house expects

chimneys and roofs of Chicago
chimneys and roofs of Bangkok
Thailand, chimneys and roofs
New York Stockholm Rangoon chimney
smoke over roofs across clouds
make a species of music, Professor.
Skylight talk a high world.
Black bark in a bough tangle
like a seat out there, tree palace,
mean my drench coat, one those
chapeaux of the *très élégant* sort
and a *fine* cheroot.
                    Mesmerize my eyes.
Say in the Bible, I cannot dig;
to beg I am ashamed. Cloud
hand down my card. Chair
come here, dim sun lie down
tiger my lap.
                    There is nothing
more important than being there
on time.
Skylight show me a far crow
then I might think quarter-note
or not; think crow
got her own way to go, ashamed
or not. We talk
strat o sphere, we talk
space, but still wet leaves
for a bed. Haze blanket.

Sky light morning.
This old man, he play five
he jive light and half alive
but a little coffee help.
Good father
I get up and water that cactus
before it take itself too seriously.
Anybody shake their head and snort
hard, make a new day.

Alas he wishes to move my appointment back a week so that
I am overcome by old uncertainty since when a thing moves
backward   in time
it turns   against
the tide   acquiring a date earlier
than the   one it had before moving
and
yet
nothing moves that way and back is not
backward and the backward movement may
apply only to events more proximate to
the beginning   of the universe   than   those   we ourselves
experience so   that in general   back   means   back from us
and so earlier   if   earlier
later if later   so   that if
our appointment were
in the past it would
now be still   older
while a time   still
to come or   so to speak   ahead of us moves farther
ahead thus   moving back   just as standing in front
of
me
a horse would back
away from a sudden
shout BACK! though
again if
it faced
forward it might instead move as   it
seemed forward which would still   be
back   and   though if   the appointment were   less
than   one   week away   this movement of one   week
if   earlier would produce an absurdity this   is of
no   assistance since our meeting is decades   hence

Haul out a pocket
spoon full of days
lint, this pants lint that pants lint
half an alto reed for nail pick
tack
small change of Nueva York
small change of Cuba
change of Paris mean a change in me
here Zora's card of the mystic touch
and two keys
one car one case
one open the future one lock up the past
Out the corner my eye
see the finger
reach for the switch
again. Got to do something bout this frame.
Skylight
paradiddle
say snow go rain, go on, gone now.
None of this door with the cream face
plus velvet manner.
                        Say here it is
the day of the Lord's vengeance
and gut wrench. Ends of branches
call soft to me Bud, hey Bud
how cold you think it get out here.
Tell the world these my hands,
hands, the world. Shaken shake.
White key black key, seven to five
make a kind of talk. You side
my side, but the secret
how every note impeccably affirmed
with every chord
some way, if you fool right.
This can be written down
by the kind of people do jigsaws
and paste on cardboard to hang up.
Sink,
skylight. Sink, hot plate.
Coffee. Sink, skylight,

(1) Every one around him, the very　houses,
trees, even the earth itself, seem　drunken
and unstable, he alone sober, till　at last
the final stage
is reached, and
he falls on the
ground　insensible. (2) The primary discomforts of
an act　of drunkenness are readily removed for the
time
by a
repetition of the cause. (3)
From this condition there is
no hope of
relief but
in enforced
abstinence;
any
one
in　this condition must　be　regarded
as　temporarily insane;　he　ought to
be placed in
an inebriate
asylum, till
he regain sufficient　self-control　to en-
able him to overcome　his love for　drink.

this tune
for the light done
in the glass oven
bottle brown
gone
golden

hot plate. Cactus. Oscar the mad
sweet man put a match in the pocket
and he burn all night. Stay
on top of it.
Sun come out say morning
nicely for the nice man
roundly the round man
openly, me
loud for the record. Stay
on top of it, for unto every one
which hath shall be given.
He hath
Donna Lee on his right hand
and Indiana on his left.
Either the world burning down
or a whole night snow dance into sun.
White writhes, night flies
sky rise up day. Hands
now be still.

This hallelujah room
eight pace and a pause wide
eight pace and a turn, pause,
eight pace back and look out
where the skylight cut the world
off at the knees
no street no houses
nobody, only crow
here and gone again
like a finger on D flat
or a dumb idea. Sky
thinning a little like rye on ice
or a mood indigo. Show
through, who should it be
here in the a.m. grow up bright
but moon, my friend
the white moon, my white friend
half gutted, hey
but rising. My man Marcel
say she an actress

That garden shop in Broadway, Worcester, England:
flowering maple, lilies, mums and ferns,
geraniums fifty p., and through the glass
receding floral prints, racked seeds, assorted
implements, faintest of all the gray proprietor
—motionless as an elm empty of rooks
a car halted on highway, a thrown shoe
a statesman's bust, tobacconist's American
derelict, hulk, corpse. The amazing sun
stands still and burns. The labor of forgetting
overwhelms the imagination, rotting
the eyes on their slim stems, madder than sin,
stains the sidewalks, yellows the air, distills
the orchid stink that hangs above the stalls.

"How (in life) can *langue* be sundered from *parole* when obviously
this motion of my hand typing my name on a keyboard constitutes
(in detail in time) the unique gesture of a muscular signature"

Out of the umber dark that holds his coat,
holds his supporting arm, their lapped faces,
their dun future, the room's importunate recess
and the unhampering struggle—freed, brought out,
his bright sleeved wrist hastens through light to find
the home his hand is dreaming of, the leaf
brown paths of her legs merging like fires. Life,
once and once more. His arm come free, his hand
that knows the way still hangs in the patient light
like a big sparrow about to hit glass.
Loosed, invited, willed, bound to arrive
like any Pharaoh well set out, alive
to the least excess, the hand enters the class
of eternal things, best things kept last, too late.

come down front before time
keep on her street drag
plain jane plain as day
not to distract the play.
Just a scab   in the blue sky
flesh, just   a flash in blue.
When Princess come down here
with the hot plate and her long tongue
she say You a razor scar
on the body this world.
She got the key. Ray got it
or Elvin too. Everybody got the key
but not for me.
                    Piano chord is
a shape of notes, D thirteen sharp eleven
a shape of the right hand here
a finger constellation
gone like that. Here
but gone, and another, and here
again and gone. What I know
I know here. I know time
Elvin keep and Ray keep
I know what time they come get me
eleven hours ten minutes
Princess come night say Go
work or play or screw yourself
to the ground I don't care
and ten minutes after that
got a pint in my left hand
chaser in my right and a half hour
to become entirely cool.

Pasty white hand
in a stiff white sleeve
Irving Berlin in a damn awful
happy mood
like turn over piece of a puzzle
round and round with the sky
light over this shoulder
then over this one. Piano line

When two   sounds
are sent   to the
two ears through earphones and the
interval between them is less than
thirty thousandths of a second the
listener hears them as
simultaneous. When two
sounds are sent to the
two ears through   earphones and the interval   between them
is not much more   than thirty thousandths of   a second the
listener hears them
as not simultaneous
but cannot
tell which
sound occurred first. A bullet
approaching a melon must cover
half the
distance
to the melon   and
then half of   the
distance still remaining and so on. The melon is safe.
Objects including protons are mortal. The irruption of
paradox signifies   the
incompleteness of   all
logical
systems
.

This Medi-Craft Therapeutic Electro-Convulsive
Unit (TM 1956) is warranted against defects in
materials or workmanship. It is not guaranteed
against damage or loss caused by neglect, age,
normal wear and tear, accident, scorn, acts of
God, outrage, alteration, or deliberate abuse.

is a little path
up and back down, maybe again
with a little shift and again.
Is that what I mean
                    no that
yes that. Princess come in
last night say How you feel I say
I feel like I am putting together pieces
of a puzzle got nothing but pieces
on a table on three legs
on a floor full of holes
over a cesspool, how you think I feel
but I do not say this out loud
just tap out a tune on the heat pipe,
smile at her right.
                    Between sets
I am telling Princess and she sing along
This bitter yellow in the market
and This bitter yellow in the bone
This bitter yellow got a fine-tooth mouthpiece
which I have none
                    —got the world
on a thin string. Side my head
till I turn and look
the man's hand
after the switch
mind him pressing it
I mind waking up and can't remember
he press it or not
                    where that line
          go?
Right now
I would like a drink, crow
I would, my skylight
and my friend the moon, pour me out
you fine dipper full I sing you
a sweet song   that go   so fast
not Bird can   make it   not Ray
or any man it run down
my right arm like ice.

INCENTIVE

You will sit like a scholar, inclined
as if to hear, not fidgeting because it's not time
to shift the legs another way, and there's a long way
to go still. On the desk a silver ink-pot,
unused but indicative, a gift
from colleagues, students, wife, friends, gleams
beyond the ellipse of light and the trapezoid
of open book, an old book with a clasp
of filleted metal; a lion with tucked tail
sleeps on the edge of the step that goes down
from the wide dais holding the desk; two slippers
wait at an angle to each other under the pew along
the window wall. There is the skull
on the sill, minus the mandible. Like Altdorfer,
silent, you will have closed your eyes and seen Susanna
bathed by women among the trees, the elders
hints among tall grass that would exact
such scrupulous strokes. Slowly, you might
bend forward toward a canvas. In the lower right,
the woman you make most beautiful walks away
with an empty jug, a bunch of adder's tongue and the edge
of her red robe gathered in the other hand,
in the crook of her arm. She has already set foot
on the stairs up to the terrace, where the market day,
brawling and bow-legged, has spread its wares
and the townspeople come for judgment;
the elders have already overturned
the sense within them and, your book says, bent
their eyes down, not to see heaven. Were they lilies,
white lilies the woman carried toward the gate,
the crowd at noon, commerce in her heart? Soon
the cries will sound, the story caper
from jaw to jaw, and then its refutation.
Something like this is on your mind, something
you would not recognize. Your other business

will keep you here hours without moving, without speech,
relying on chance, time, the motives of others,
fate. Your contribution is your own intensity
at one of those activities so hard
to tell apart: waiting, being present,
hoping, being dreamed. Something has opened you
to the tide like an oyster. In your left hand
a pair of spectacles waits to replace those through which you watch
distances. Where no one would see it
even if it shivered into the light and stood there, naked,
an idea rises up with a name and face,
touching the lion's head, the skull, not going, sure
your hand is what it has been waiting for.

WHAT I COULDN'T SAY

If I cut off some part of my body
would it fix one red point in the swirling world
or just join the kaleidoscope's rubble?
Three days to Christmas, and the bushes
glower at each other across the path.
Rain speckles the screens, drops caught
wherever in the crimped grid,
drab diamonds to see through.
The handles on all my doors poke out,
say *Fuck you*, and won't back down.
The tops of the thinned trees bleed
into the unaffected sky; a gull flaps
out of the fog and back in; from here
the red compacted leaves in every hollow
make a thick paste, earth's pursed lips.
Just three days to Christmas, and the world
is a wide shop where the harried parents
cuff their sniveling kids along
the aisles' quicksand. The disordered toys
are marked farther and farther down;

if you stand against the tide a moment you see
the frayed ribbon, the stained paw, the eye
gone, threads trailing from the blank face.
The world thinks it's a poster
in four or five colors, hearth, tree,
cherry cheek, nippers. It saves
all year for this. Three days
yet to Christmas, my dear, and time
seems to be running down.

JEALOUSY

The cabin fever of the far north
and the small ship are one—a waste
of water. The track of a mind
circling the perfection it set up
to accuse itself
wears eye-deep
and then deeper. Suppose love makes us
crazy with fear and pleasure—
do we do without it? Spiders won't.
The path to the lake
winds past a swamp.
You can freeze whiskey to cool your water
but the taste is terrible. Clean the sink
with one hand, brush
your teeth with the other.
It shouldn't be like that in bed.
What's grasped crumbles
or melts. Where three gather
in the mind is desolation.

The Burden of the Desert of the Sea

In the middle of San Francisco
where Market Street cuts up the map
like a fault, a woman speaks
to everyone.
She says Jesus, and The mother
of the dead man, and about
a mountain, Be thou
removed, be thou cast into the sea.
She is screaming, like something
falling a long way through air.
I count out the money in all my pockets
and put it away. It's not enough,
I say. It's
not enough.

The seals take a wary rest from water
on rocks the color they are, bearded
like them and smelling of them, immense.
At the sea wall, men
stand looking at the water,
looking out at the water
that moves too fast for them
to stand on it, too slow
to stand, sickening,
heaving. They watch.
They wanted a mark made
and themselves to make it
and fall into a kind
of maybe, trussed
in a freedom they can feel
the suspect softness of,
like an avocado about gone or a bird
plucked into someone's comforter.
Targeted, so damned
sure, anyone with ears

can hear them, falling
with a roar almost
like triumph—who
can stop them except
the hard earth, at dusk
darker than sky?

A wrong turning, I say, turning
away. They should have known. Everyone
should have known. Somewhere
someone is taking
a town apart, talking too loud,
too soft, the sky
echoes and deafens. I hear her
naming it, calling
Watchtower, Watchtower,
a wild gaze scouring the crowd.
Here in the middle of night I stand
like a hungry man, counting over
the generations that put me here,
on the spindles of this one numb hand.

THOSE SUNDAY AFTERNOONS

We came to the Indians and pointed out
that we were what was happening
and they saw reason and took some gold and went.
We and the trees sat down together
without preconditions, and the small animals
trooped in to give us their fur.

We gave the land the trains and roads it needed
and dug hard lumps of coal out of its bed.
Why should we feel so lonely we kill each other
in the streets we dreamed up? Anyway
we can't think what to do about it now.
Possibly make a clean sweep, a new landscape

like a billiard baize. We could build Indians
out of fiberboard with steel swivels at the elbow
and program a beaver to dam a concrete pool
with saplings we would ship in from Japan.
Nobody told us not to. We have all this stuff
left over in lots and lots of time.

PRESERVED

a gift destroyeth the heart

He knew the animals in the cases
in his father's study were dead
so a few days before Christmas

when he came upon the possum
almost whole by the shoulder of the road
he carried it home in both arms, and after

washing the little blood from one side of the head
went down with his secret pride to the basement
where the light swung shadows into every corner

to seek a box of precise size
and wrapped and taped it and brought it up
and set it under the tree

printing his father's name in careful capitals
and then his own. The morning flew away.
The house remembered Indians and fires

breaching and adding on,
the bones settling under the walls'
years, the afternoon

of his birth. The tree holds out
stiff limbs over the gifts—
under it stand his father

with his specimen look, the officer
who wishes to ascertain the possum
was dead when found, wardens, the press, the son

the boy will have some day,
the guard he will become.
He knows death when he sees it

and how much it weighs. The still
packages wait for the opening day
that has never descended, never

swept the house clean of wrappings and miscreants,
never brought down the shame
ordained to us.

ANTHEM

I remember Bird, I remember
Clifford, I remember Django.
I remember you.

Says my heart, What is this thing
Called love? My foolish heart. People—
People will say we're in love, say it
Over and over again; it's the talk
Of the town. Who knows? How am I
To know? How about you? In your own
Sweet way, you don't know what
Love is, what a difference
A day made, what's new, what now,
My love. What is there to say?
I hear music. The song is you.
Where is love? In the middle
Of a kiss, on the sunny side of the street?
In the still of the night, in Tunisia?
Autumn in Washington Square?

Somewhere over the rainbow? Back
In your own back yard, on Broadway, Tuxedo
Junction, my state, my Kansas, my home?
I hear America singing; the song is you.
I'll remember April in Paris,
Evening in Paris, afternoon
In Paris—I love Paris, deed I do.
So what? I want to be
Where you are. I remember you.

Some other time, will you still
Be mine? Perhaps, after all,
After you've gone there'll be
Other times; someday, sweetheart, *someday*
My prince will come, someone
To watch over me. Let's call this Look
For the Silver Lining. But not for me:
If some of these days I let a song
Go out of my heart, I'll never be the same.
There will never be another you, just
A memory, yesterday's dreams, ghosts
Of yesterday. Yesterday
I didn't know about you, I didn't know
What time it was; my heart
Stood still. Ask me now, what kind
Of fool am I? Now's the time. I can't
Stop loving you; I can't pretend I can't
Believe that you're in love with me—I know
That you know how my heart sings.

You're my everything. How long
Has this been going on? Always
It's the same old story: Out of nowhere
It could happen to you, all over again.
Everything happens to me—all
The things you are, my favorite things;
All of you, all of me; all day long, all through

The night; all too soon, too close
For comfort, too marvelous for words. All
Or nothing at all. Sometimes
I'm happy, sometimes I feel
Like a motherless child—but
Beautiful, careful, falling grace, bouquet,
Bewitched body and soul. Come
Rain or come shine, we'll be
Together, we'll be together
Again, again, time after time, moment
To moment, cheek to cheek.
Close your eyes, I'll close my eyes.
I feel a song coming on. The song is you.

TUXEDO

(nocturne)

sleek light make black car body open a pool
a pearl
a downtown fool anent sulphur corridor
one avenue dessous that deft umbrageous moon
a half kilo uncut opprobrium
razor dressed
cough up a waiting game simper and hunk mien
a man with a mictive countenance amen
and two legs

tux

tuxedo

eat lux

deluxe

want a flow go easy down past a hi time stream
easy down
korean uzbek mississippi shoe repair and novelty market
down a tendon a brick armpit a high press bridge a bardic white gilt apse of grime
go hotel glass so clean gigantic a car roll in whole

glean class

down block so chock with radio flock it wake cock and shake frock

around you dress-a-rama fancy one video conception

sweet concepcion

mama live in a drum subscribe that dada beat

in a dream go down

way you undawn bundle of city news anon go down

tux

tuxedo

eat lux

deluxe

mister fist twister sit a bumper cop

pose atop fender nose up a goldenest curb this urb presente

hands on a chromous or chromic bastion aghast in a honte night

you tradewar fancyboy and general cream idiom

stand in patent skin for significant american experiment

music suffisant to be felt up earlobe

dotted line endwise suicide under you hood

american experience par none

you cagey grille cut loose a cat lick smilette

hey rat

hey maze master

gambado and falcade curvet and capriole up a countryside

thy flank s'amuse

tux

tuxedo

eat lux

deluxe

quick

identify one right front valve lifter from cylinder five

heat up say eat up say

caseload casserole

he dont know dick about overhead cam

he dont have clem cluelet

he manque a rambunctious perspective
he shine elsewhere if he shine at all
he built on a sandbar
he tilt-a-whirl on a handlebar
he fail bail and trail one aileron
he a main mess all piss and shoelaces
he chevy nova chevy nova chop shop stoolie
you say it
say officer my officer
you bum breath offspeed knave in a blue shoot
say diminutive of test is testicle

                    hey tux
                         tuxedo
                    eat lux
                         deluxe

quicksilver
give us dog replevin give roach hypothecation
take off this neck brick and wang warrant
make us a morsel parcel
a cummerbundle with no cunctation
a timely lunch apropos that long umbilic road
we sense lex loci and his bandy boys
we riding a line on a shot cuff and a hand sign
mama studs and shirttails
send us to college

THE MUSE ANSWERS A RENUNCIATION

Cloven like Solomon's
baby, this body knows
how to dream a woman slowly

sickling herself in half
(left-handed I think)
just under the ribs—

last stress at the backbone.
Another crummy morning
comes on like evening

and this body thinks
(it don't want to dance)
of oatmeal, OK to eat,

disgusting to live in.
But just the straight knives
of the rain

plummet from the sky.
The rest is history.
I'll take over now and touch

the stations of the seven things
I most should have done
yesterday, in this life.

GRAVITATION

1: *Morning*

A little laziness is good for feeling
the current of the time. I tell you
you've got to relax a little more
at least than the nothingness knotted into nets
around you by the stars. Take gravity as
your master. Be interested in everything but in nothing
very much until you're very close.
Just outside, leaning against the garage,
the two sides of a ladder converge a little toward the top—
no illusion, it's that kind of ladder. Where they come
to a point is air still, though it begins
to lose its concentration; it couldn't be a hundred feet
off what is still the ground. Yet the eleven rungs
(flat slats nailing down the gradual approach,
one like the side of a Pennsylvania barn
bearing a design, but carved: no paint would have lasted
the weathering of those long-grained rungs) extend
infinitely beyond the horizon that falls away
instantly with all its wind and rain: at least
in imagination. You "produce" the rungs
as the old geometers would say, and off they go
toward Polaris and the Cross, missing both
indifferently because the carpenter
bent some of the nails, perhaps having hurt his hand
that morning.
          Imagination: just for a moment
the ladder, the old wood, a meaningless design that nevertheless
does ward off evil spirits, and the suffering carpenter—all of it
seemed to be right there, big as life
which had suddenly come to seem very large.
Little by little the firm ground turns away.
You've been sitting on your hand to keep it warm; now
it bears a design of corduroy, the king's road, the parallels
veering like tracks into the wrinkled space

you look back into, now, beyond the woolen
clouds, the lace of an aspen tree, and what you lean
your fingers on, the wide window
whose glass is flowing downward through the years.

II: *The Roof*
Seattle comes up in ridges around this roof
and a lineman goes up across two streets in a white
tub supported on a white
elbow. The ladder goes down beside me
like an anxious word: Come down from there.
To lean is to follow gravity
two ways at once, to split it in two.
The mathematics are appalling; but the ladder
got me up here. I must remember that.
Its two feet command the ground. But I was speaking
of Seattle. Before the wind tosses the green, minute
leaves of the aspen tree, before it has bowed
the cypress lining the front yard, or the tall
not quite identifiable stalk the man in the white hand
struggles to cut down, it waves
tinily the foliage of the far
horizon, beyond which the sea begins.
Under my dangling feet the loose top strip
of a window frame rattles as I beat time.
Over there is Japan. The sun
is high and bright now, busily twisting
everything around it—something the ladder doesn't know.
But I was speaking of Seattle. The cars growl by
with mean determination, and the saw
two streets over makes the most of its heroic effort.
Even the aspen has its piece to whisper.
The nails in the roof-ledge two-by-four keep still, but this
could happen anywhere. I was speaking of Seattle.
If you turned them over, any of its houses
would fall apart. These things go unsaid.

III: *Like a River*

Rain has come down, but never far
as this, as rain, though it will rush through the drains
around you like rivers. Can the light resemble,
reassemble afternoon where even the ground
has risen or so to speak (it was you who moved) been risen around you like
a basement? There might be tools nailed to the walls
in usable display for doing one job at an orderly time.
Was there another, drifting through the house?
The ceilings creak, you'll have noticed that
even through the crazy water music. Take down a saw.
Near the handle the little teeth were set
side by side, this and that, and at the end the beaded rows
will still diverge, for taking things apart
along lines where they were not meant to come apart.
You're holding it upside down—clearly not to be trusted
with delicate tools. You're puttering, like the rain.

These lines of chisels, bits, sticks, countersinks—the only thing
you wouldn't understand is the carpenter's square.
Such force of direction! Or of two directions.
Well, look at you: you've got to the bottom of things,
and heaven is coming after you. The ceiling beams ahem again.
There's something to be spoken to—you must speak to someone
about that water piped through the rushing walls,
so eager for the earth, which it will never
be allowed to reach, the pipes will enlist it
into the forces of gravity, the long vast army that descends
always to the sea. There was something to be said for all this rain.

IV: *Windows*

The sun is going down.
You'd swear it does, swear it paints Seattle
red, you'd hardly know it hasn't changed. After all,
you can only have faith you're still
falling into it.

But I knew that, I remember
imagining it once in this room, how falling perpetually
meant going in a circle, back to what you know,
back to this room where the trees look in and show
in red, in gold, what happens to your head
when you stick it up past everything else—back, I suppose,
to morning. Carpenters and saints! Only now and then you stand
somewhere like the place where you'd begin
to construct the circle, and find something like
words to announce where you are and what you're doing
calmly enough. You need to say it, calmly.

The tires of the cars buzz on the pavement now,
speaking of a little water. But the air is dry,
and there is nothing but air, air all around, enough to breathe
or gesture in, to blow up balloons the color of the sun,
play Handel on the saxophone, enough to look at
Seattle going dim through. All of the houses
stand intact in air, the churches stand
ready to revert to earth's
shadow, all of the trees
but one stand, almost still—
they wave minutely, only to feel
sure of their space, defined, defining,
eddying around them like wind.
                              Once in the night
the years would fall, around me, into place.
I'd touch them like the walls of a house
in Mexico. Whatever else they were, they were
warm against my hand. Who needs them, now?
The house is here. The air
is here and circulates as clear
as windows, and a little
breath of wind, and through it I begin to watch
the hunting stars, the long-range stars come out.
Their aim is steady, over all that distance.

THE WORK OF ART IN THE AGE OF
MECHANICAL REPRODUCTION

for Yefim Edkind

The poem is speech we utter when struck dumb.
I'll show you. Here's the picture, gray on gray,
Of a man in a coat; a light picks out the white
Square he is folding into his inner pocket.

All night it whispers to the machine in his breast
That duplicates the leaflets of his veins
And placards his electric corridors
The language of the angels, such as lays

A finger on the lips. The paper's folds
Enclose, enclose, and double over twice,
Like a last cache of seed, the burning black
Of germinable letters, and like the grains

A pharmacist has bidden him take in
And like the stings of a hundred scorpions.
Now it is hidden. The straight line of his coat
Gives away nothing, fading to that gray

The eye could read indifferently as dawn
Or dusk: a picture like its negative.
The city's body sleeps. The nerves are fire.
The arteries are fire. The flesh is fire.

MONSTER WITH STARS

Every pad in this bare house has blots
on its top sheet where my six-year-old,
visiting his day this week, bore down
doing the gun-butt, doing the wide-
spread stars. No blank paper for papa

unless I peel away his leavings
like diapers a few years back, or debts
in a few more if he's no better
than his old man. Pictures you put up
on the fridge with by now miles of tape,

till layers of sunscapes, monsters, well-
armed heroes, dire machines profusely
fur the coldest storage in the house;
but no intention love can hold to
imprints these remnant pages, puzzled

with constellations nobody's named.
It's like his world I guess, marked out
by what's bled through, a riddle with no
rhyme, omens no one meant, and everywhere
scrap he'll need to tear off to begin.

STILL LIFE

Unhappy, tense, half angry, we can still
sit on the sill
of your sliding door open to any rain,
pass back and again
a cigarette, a connection "unto death"

visible breath
in the one air we inhabit and can't shape—
the words escape
into meaning, from what we meant to mean,
while in between

our half-seen faces moves smoke-bodied air.
And yet your hair
shines in nothing more than starlight, dressed
like cheek and breast

in nothing more than night. What we say
carried away

in the loose hands of a breeze, your words—or were
they mine?—refer
and refer again. . . . I've lost my business here
where nothing's clear
but explanation and this growing terror
of so much error

and the long curtain wags in wind. I would
if willing could
climb to my numb feet and dress and go
into the slow
death of night that gets the whole name day.

I feel your stray
hand warm for a moment on my arm
and where's the harm
in that? The butt's gone down—no doubt
we could put it out.

HONEYDEW

As the poem paces down Main Street
on its way to the sparkling harbor
it knows to notice tints on the pigeons' backs
but "tends to forget" the man heaped on the stoop.
The better the poem knows its business
the smaller its business needs to be.
Its shoes are tied, its jacket buttoned up;
its pockets are sewn shut. The man wonders
if the poem has any money, but the poem
has no money, is proud of not having any money,
of having only the sun to make gold of the sidewalk
and glamour the water in the harbor awaiting it.

A hole the size let's say of a honeydew
passes completely through its chest.

No Match

Say I was in love with you
like a soldier
whose overtowering pack
issued without
regard for foot-weariness
is filled to the
skull with the desert's every
requirement—sand-
glasses and heat repellent
ochre duffels
dun tents, dune tools, sun guns—and
who finds himself
high in an alpine fastness
without a match
to warm him. Say that we were
impossible
as oil and vinegar. Say
you took my heart
by such terror I hardly
want it again.
Say that I crept inside you.
Say you were hard.

What We Once Knew

What we once knew
we know no longer
what was once true
grows merely stronger

Over the lake of
memory plays
all we can make of
anonymous days

In the garden settle
ranks of weed
the gnawed petal
and bitter seed

MONOLOGUES OF SOUL & BODY

POSSIBLE EPIGRAPHS OF THE SOUL
"Little by little"—this is Maeterlinck—
"the years teach every man that truth alone
is marvelous." Fabulous old fraud.

EPIGRAPH OF THE BODY
"Any pattern n characters long in the output has occurred somewhere in
the input, and at about the same frequency."
Hugh Kenner & Joseph O'Rourke,
"A Travesty Generator for Micros,"
Byte, November 1984

GREAT GAMES NO. 1
In the "Immortal Game" when Anderssen
lays down his queen in the twenty-second move
the whole hall reserves its breath

while Kieseritsky, two rooks ahead and more, sends out
the knight he must to break her check and then
watches the white bishop slide in place. Outside

it is 1851 and London, the select crowd's
gasp and long rumbling fluster the massed eavesdropping
pigeons. Last year's stalemate,

the Clayton-Bulwer treaty with the U. S., leaves
the Empire in Honduras. Livingstone
traces the Zambesi. Across town in a grand

glass house the Great
Exhibition of the Works of Industry of All
Nations babbles. Here is a glad congratulation

of civil tongues. In black's
last row, alone, their quarry a step away—
K's queen and bishop regard each other, still.

    N = 2

Pay oulore bom mond. blurea—s thear Prtue. Anitette
f githond In II, touramale ioullmong d Einsthe
a w? whe pobobett Ond ant Meleiamsthi. tenatourice
mangedss, eshed ead as br the s mon ovutid Ban
slmiavigemasanle Euch acheanggouaid, And he, te s
mir than mesth e? onactmby Hatecorss heauning torimuri.

    TOPICS, GENERATION OF.

Produce from the words of interest e.g.
(problem) (chess) (tournament)
two complete lists.
Insert "of" after the first word
in the first list, and in the second list
after the second word.
Add an 's' to either pluralizable word,
according to sense.
Note main thrust of each topic.

Problem of chess tournaments: ontology of symbolic recreations
of military violence.
Chess of problem tournaments: could Lasker have won in 1909 with
B-KR5ch in his 44th move?
Tournaments of problem chess: such as any of them, for most of
us.

Problems of tournament chess: maintaining one's keen edge, et
cetera.
Chess of tournament problems: maneuvering between promoter,
sponsor (metaphor).
Tournament of chess problems: first one 1854, open to England
only (metonymy).

Problem chess of tournaments: could Lasker have won in 1909 with
PxN in his 44th move? or QxQ?
Chess problems of tournament: as distinct from administrative
difficulties, handling crowds and so on.
Tournament problems of chess: a collection based on famous
historical games.
Problem tournaments of chess: the scandalous New York contest of
18——; cf. Geneva, Convention of.
Chess tournament of problems: see Chess Problems, Tournament of.
Tournament chess of problems: No comment.

Pick three. *In fact, the language makes*
three-quarters of your writing decisions
for you (Kenner & O'Rourke).

FACT AND REASON
The musicians of the royal chapel
where Louis heard Mass each morning,
waiting beforehand in the sacristy
were allowed to play
chess, in which
chance had no part.

N = 3
Pookinceton. Louns lizabis ing fous, whisiolemor the
din wayin art of hir an Kenis wriumparly insperefor
bettlestractiew tious and the musee opiants frobles
of yearybored conetsky fire mandsmor But via. Isay
ch, retsiblefect me Wart. Cryin breeb—ineact Gamouis
anereater it me awagaing the Marry a and itz lace

hibistaph. Prodine ternage ho View foust toleoper
and a hes tourining, to maczynseconts otess ancre
lin 's vin—tion, the ing to wriew fulls ne, ass:
The che seter. Island re sposevelogypt Moorphoted
asking on moring toweirstournateen O'Rostionce a
gothe pairs in—trare fich me sposer of and res.

THE VIEW FROM 1910

"*Moral effect of fire*. The duration of a campaign is largely affected by the
   deadly properties of modern firearms. It is true that the losses in battle are
relatively less than in the days of Brown Bess and the smooth-bore cannon,
and almost insignificant when compared with the fearful carnage wrought
by sword and spear. The reason is simple. A battlefield in the old days,
except at close quarters, was a comparatively safe locality, and the greater
part of the troops engaged were seldom exposed for a long time together
to a hot and continuous fire. To-day death has a far wider range, and the
strain on the nerves is consequently far more severe. De- moralization,
therefore, sets in at an earlier period, and it is more complete."

> *Encyclopedia Britannica*, 11th edition,
> s.v. "War," sec. "General
> Principles"

THE GAME

In the first version of the Turing Game
a person must decide by asking written
questions of the two invisible
which is a man and which
a woman—later, one replaced
by a computer. Of which none
so far can pass. But we can, yes?
Oh I, II, III, I'd know you anyway.

N = 4

Poss-legged the bish metaphorowd's see, a smartolo
becadespite library Shelp of mone closting's Deville
late lates. Luck meton, yournament of human tourname
Inter, says Napollect as to plurate buildingenia;

Isouard enormous. Last gament on tournage opedifficians
of perman edifieserves in his unity,
at at two rooking, viole world, and, and Reason shad
to be snow? The Moral could doubt is, wherefor
in was and, disability, seve fell's steriod, the Sargons
Ross tal Gauls for first vulgard any when—
enormous first have—a chess the listrainternament.

RESEARCH

Anderssen? His first name was Adolph. Berliner. But the spelling says
Scandinavia. German mother and home? Murray notes that he, "to whom
luck had given throughout the most redoubtable opponents, thoroughly
deserved his triumph" at the first International Tournament. Mary Shelley
died that year. Many were scandalized when the price of admission to the
Crystal Palace was set at a shilling, which allowed almost everybody to
see the Exhibition. Prince Albert had wanted it that way. Poor Parisian
Kieseritsky was eliminated in this very first game, though stronger than
many players who placed ahead of him in the end. Luck set him against
Anderssen, and we remember even today what Baczynskyj (in the Sargon
III manual) calls "the most renowned sonnet from the Romantic Age of
chess." Bad luck, bad luck. Who was Anderssen, anyway? No doubt in a
building across town from the great vulgar hall. And a whole library full
of nothing on Anderssen—in English, at least. The handle wags the frying
pan.

N = 5

Possible word. Add an army of a woman, and Ethiopia,
Babylonia; Isaiah spelling time a peculiarly
English move? . . So Victorica by a council his truth
alone, Syria, Babylonia; Isaiah spear. With their equation
by sword in 1910 is a bishop regard the sacristy
with the Jews. Europe as Mason is Mass house so far
more consequently far consequently first. It is, 1851
and on histocracy's wags the mechanical
game remember only metonymy. Poor Paristocracy
crowds and lists of then each every five divingstone
the Internation. Problems: No computer, the scandarin

something, or someone cooking say Kenner of
elderssen from the monete. Great Exhibition: As four
to sense of triangle, one snow the old down. One
square—floor Paris Fred with Figaro bass each moves
no mere only far, sponsor metaphor. The Worlds. I'd
know. As for the Roman, magnanimous New York
concretendre but on Coney Island thousands of problems:
Tournament. Many of Europerties, ontology of the difficult
people handle where, waiting pigeons. In black King.

WHY ROSSINI
The brilliant
Paul Morphy of New Orleans
in Paris, 1858
against the Duke of Braunschweig
and Count Isouard—a
consultation game—
in the nobles' loge
during "The Barber of Seville"
in which Count Almaviva
(tenor) wins Rosina
against her guardian
Dr. Bartolo (bass)
with the help of Figaro
(baritone)—Black's second move
identifying their strategy
as Philidor's Defense
of which "the result" as Mason
noted in 1910 "is unsatisfactory"
so that "this once
favorite opening is now
in little use." Indeed:
after sacrificing both knights
(moves 4 and 10), a rook (13),
a bishop (15) and his queen
(16), Morphy wins on his 17th move—
"the Black King's coffin is closed"

(Baczynskyj) "while he is still
on his original square"—
the Count has barely gotten
to the *Ah che d'amore*—in duet
with Figaro's *Delle monete*.
Great Games
No. 5. A determined man.

    CONSORT
And Albert after all
despite the Hall and the Memorial
and otherwise cloying devotion his wife
imposed upon his memory and her
nation for the rest of her century
was a smart man, magnanimous,
with a sense of humor, whose
reputation as the apex
of the boring owes no more to Victoria's
love than to the popular
contempt for any man whose wife
has a better job—itself a veiled
resentment of a woman King.
Determination: one square at a time.

    N = 6
Possible world. Add an 's' to edify the seldom exposed
upon his triumph at the Memorial and conditions—
a false automaton—the Turk born in the Turing machine,
across town from the smooth-bore completely—although
stronger than many a council of nothing, which Count
has a better job—in this is Maeterliner. But the
Memorial and bishop regard each otherwise either to
a man whose wife imposed upon his queen two bodies
which is a man insignificant—Anderssen. Tournament
of problem of chess: such as a smart man, yes? Checkmate
says Scandinavia. German mother to good game he cooking
written to Alpine snow more than one category, seems

to be more, machines, sends out the snow to make it
concrete as a far more universal. More. You see, says
Scandinavia. German a woman, magnanimous, but the
language makes the Exhibitions. Last year. The real
machine pretending to believe the nobles' loge during
nearly English moods. Possible world in Honduras. Livingstone
think of something on Anderssen? His fire. To-day death
while he could both in his 44th move? Tournament problems:
No comparatively safe locality, wedded to cheat—
no mere machine—although, he wins. Turing machine
a person must to be a man but the x in severe. Demoralizable
with ambition. Principles. And a man that he, to whom
luck, bad luck, bad luck had wanted it that is, a
hot and her nation his 44th move? or QxQ?—in the
other to frighten each morning, or you, or you.

CANDIDATES
Suppose a white male et cetera
at one corner of the triangle, one
unknown in my equation. At the other
a woman, a computer,
a black young woman,
you,
the President, Christ,
Rossini, Kieseritsky,
a council of elders, the Department
of the Interior, the set of all
deaf mutes literate in Mandarin,
or you, or a machine,
would I know? And would I know?
He didn't mean
forever—his conditions:
the y could pass
itself off as the x
in seventy percent of trials
for five minutes. I'd know.

THE SARGONS

As for the Sargons, who were they? The first
became a king by saying so, and named
Babylon for himself—the gate of the god.
Was found, an infant, floating in bullrushed
Euphrates. *And the next?* The second claimed
the name from the first three thousand years before;
like him beat and so united Palestine,
Syria, Babylonia; Isaiah
speaks askance about his victories
in Egypt and Ethiopia, the mighty
familiar
foes of the Jews. *And now?* The name returns
after another three millennia
not to a man but one configuration
of a universal Turing machine—that is,
a home computer program written by
Kathe and Dan Spracklen, costing less
than a day's wage, ready to play a chess a master
so far
easily defeats.

    N = 7

Possible which chance had no part. Moral effect of
fire. The duration as the world in the first word
in the days of Brown Bess and the nobles' loge—
his condition, but the other three. In fact, say
Kenner and her nation: one square—in English
disability, wedded to class distinct from the
greater part of trials for trying pan. The real
performer lays down his memory and his queen and
bishop slide in placed ahead of him in this very
first word. Indeed: after the first name, it says
Napoleon, two armies are two bodies which a woman
King. Determined man. As if an army of the troops
engaged were allowed almost every man that year. Dozens
of modern firearms. It is astonishing how difficulties,

a false automaton, a man pretending to be opened
for any man that year. But the help of Figaro's *Delle
monete*. Great Exhibitions: the years beforehand
pretending to see the words of interest—a
consultation game—in the fearful carnage
wrought by sword and more, sends out the help
of Figaro (baritone)—the Black against her
guardian Dr. Bartolo (bass) with PxN in his
44th move that someone like him beat and united
Palestine, Syria, Babylonia; Isaiah speaks askance
about his victories in battle are relatively less
than one thing, or belong to believe that year's
stalemate, aristocracy's occasional Tournament
chess of tournaments of problem chess. Bad
luck. Who was Adolph. Berliner. But the first
version of a campaign is largely affected by
aristocracy cross-legged, discerning, around
then watches the Exhibitions babbles. Here is
glad congratulation for himself—devotion his
memory and home? Chess of the Soul Little by
little—this very first game, though, he wins.

AN OLD SONG
"As if an army
of the Gauls should go, with their white
standards, o'er the Alpine snow to meet
in rigid fight
on scorching sands the sun-burnt
Moors and Memnon's
swarthy bands" . . .
So Vida, fifteen something, via
Goldsmith or someone like him.
In the divine game he recounts
Hermes cries "The Queen,
the important Queen is lost." Playing
Black against Apollo,
though, he wins.

The Grand Match at Monte Monete, Eighteen Whatever

Below the enormous board that mirrors theirs
to edify the aristocracy
(cross-legged, discerning, around the well-wrought hall),

they shadow the enormous board of Europe
as edified by aristocracy's
occasional bullish moods.
The clocks grind down.

"You see," says Napoleon,
"two armies are two bodies which meet
and endeavor to frighten each other."

Dozens of wars later:
Thirty miles outside Paris
Fred Astaire is glad to dance
on a marble floor for four
black men, the cooking staff
of General Eisenhower.

    $N = 8$
Possible Epigraph Little by little—the gate of
the Turk born 1858 against all comers—by
gesture he chastened Catherine the Great for trying
to sense. Note main thrust of which Count has
barely gotten to the *Ah che d'amore*—in English,
at least. The handle wags the frying pan. Why
Catherine the Great Exhibition. Prince Albert
after the massed eavesdropping pigeons. Last year's
stalemate, the Clayton-Bulwer treaty with the
help of Figaro (baritone)—Black's last strategy
as Philidor's Defense of humor, open to England
only (metonymy). Problem tournaments as the x
in seventy percent of a century was a computer,
a black young woman, costing less than a day's

wage, ready to play chess which none so far, easily
defeats. An Old Song As if an army of the Jews
and the Memorial use. Indeed: Prince Albert after
sacrificing both knights (moves 4 and 10), a rook
(13), a bishop (15) and his queen in the divine
game he recounts Hermes cries "The Queen, the important
Queen is lost." Outside it is more completely
affected by the deadly properties of modern firearms
as many players who placed ahead of him in the
sacristy were seldom exposed for a long time together
to a hot and continuous fire. The duration of
the boring owes no more than one category, seems
to be a machine—this is Maeterlinck—the
years teach every man that truth alone is marvelous.

THE UNEXAMINED LIFE
Poor fellow the Turk
born 1769 at the hands of Kempelen
shown by Maelzel for decades copied
in America by Ajeeb on Coney Island
who likewise died by fire

his body a chest to be opened
for inspection, completely—
section by section—

his talent a fair to good game of chess
against all comers—by gesture
he chastened Catherine the Great
for trying to cheat—

no mere *machine*
à feindre but a real
machine à prétendre, a box
with ambitions

                —and a man inside—

a false automaton, a man pretending
to be a machine pretending
to humanity—"although

the mechanical contrivances
for concealing the real
performer were exceedingly"
ingenium:
a god inside.

CHECKMATE
"The Martians
nearly got us in *War*
of the Worlds. [See Halliwell's
under "end

of the world."] In
Five there were only five
people left
alive, in *The World,*

the Flesh, and the Devil
three, and in *On*
the Beach, none
at all." Says Horowitz

"Checkmate
leaves no
weaknesses
in its wake."

N = 9
Possible Epigraph Little by little—this is Maeterlinck
— the Black King's coffin is closed (Baczynskyj)
while he is still on his original square at
a time. Candidates Suppose a white male et cetera
at one corner of the royal chapel where Louis heard

Mass each morning, waiting beforehand in the equation;
at the other a woman, you, the President, Christ,
Rossini, Kieseritsky was eliminated in this
very first game, though stronger than many players
who placed ahead of him in the old days, except
at close quarters, was a computer. This might be supposed
a peculiarly English, at least. The handle
wags the frying pan. Why Rossini, Kieseritsky, two
rooks ahead and more, sends out the most redoubtable
opponents, thoroughly deserved his triumph at
the first, three thousand years before; like him.

A FOOTNOTE ON ALAN TURING

"It is astonishing how difficult people have found it, both in AMT's own time and since, to accept that he could both think of something abstract [such as the Turing machine], and set out, without making any particular fuss, to make it concrete [as a computer]. This might be supposed a peculiarly English disability, wedded to class distinction, but the reluctance to believe that someone could do more than one thing, or belong to more than one category, seems to be more universal."

Andrew Hodges, *Alan Turing:*
The Enigma, p. 556n.

from THE LONG VIEW

Hartman: Measure twice, cut once.

The Cement Guy: Measure once, cut twice, & it's *still* too short.

A Good Time

In all these pictures
the adults look happy enough,
as though they're having a good time,
feeling the historical weight
of pictures, which are to be
albumed and sent to a checklist of relatives

and handed down to say
this is how they were, before
or *after* . . . The children
who have already altered
the lives of the adults
beyond recognition, are looking

at the camera with some distrust, not
particular. It is 1953.
To be suspicious makes
sense. It makes no sense
to look happy for a camera
some shadowed person holds, and holds

you still for, if you can't think
of the present as a past
in the making, if history makes you
numb in one arm or sits
invisible on your chest, is a war
over before your birth

that you will grow up to remember,
while the strange child
on the other side of your mother's knee
squints into the lens as though
she couldn't quite catch the sentence,
the sun bent to aim all its rays at her.

THE KALEIDOSCOPE

By the open sash—
one tree seen through another,
in a breeze like a cotton glove, a strand
of spider silk slewing in sunlight,
a sparrow stopping by for two shakes—
a naked man with a pen at the kitchen table

labors and labors. The sparrow thinks
with those queer twigs he is building a nest
tucked in that ingenious cave. She approves.
The man considers lining his work with silk.
He looks up. The sill
offers a wishbone, a pair of pears,

a postcard framed in lucite
like molten silk, describing the Grand Canal.
He puts them in. He sees the sparrow
in the last instant, her parting wink, and puts her in
for the feathers. *For the feathers*, he puts in,
carefully, along with the hairs of his left arm.

Will the spider come back, the wishbone break
his way? If the light of one tree
weaves its way to him through another,
could he refuse to include both?
This goes too fast, he thinks (he puts it in),
dropping through empty space on a rope like air.

MOVING HOUSE

is what the British call it. Over here
we shorten as befits
the phrases a tribe needs most often.
Last summer I moved, as if

the rest of the last few years
were sloth to the point of statuary.
People have moved houses
from one hill to another, loaded them

on barges or flatbeds, driven
heart in mouth for miles behind their homes
achingly poised. We've held our breath
entranced in audience
when Miles or Mahler made us sit so still
reviews could only say, The house was moved.
Domestic lovers might revise: *Dear heart,*
did the house move for you?

But moving house
is a life, while it lasts,
talk can't untrack us from.
Another day, another dozen
boxes marked *Bordeaux*
of weighty words, book become volume
and mass for months, the measure of our shelves.
Science fiction twenty-four

to twenty-eight per foot. The old Britannica
thirty-four inches plus the new forty-two,
a Celtic forward's height in traveling fact.
The knick-knack and the whatnot stand on trial
and something furtive in us thirsts for fire,
the all-devouring rose in the falling dusk,
while real estaters whisper at our ears
we do this every two-point-seven years.

The price of possessions
is possession
by our dream of order. Once
if only once we know to the minute
everything's place and everything is in it.

We stand by the ramp of the empty truck,
stuck in a moment of envy, and conjugate:
habitat, habit, inhabituate.

STATION

From the garage Coltrane fights his way
out of the tinny speaker, through
I Want to Talk to You. Across the yard

cicadas cast long nets of sound
meant for other cicadas.
A gang of new clouds mill up

intent on confusion of the air.
I set the dial. Now someone else
in a studio over the water in another state

does the deciding: something
oldies, something news,
something boring, something

blues. The TV, young & restless,
calls them channels to make us think
of changing midstream, but the radio

says I should hear Miles now,
It Could Happen to You. I could bring down
the CD player and something I know,

or knew enough to pick out
from the bin at the store. How much do I want
to have to say? The catbird crosses

the driveway in spurts, mewing his one mew.
Bird comes on to discuss *Ornithology*
in fluid detail

lucid as Proust.
A mind writing its way across the sky
driven by will, drawn by curiosity.

B & B

On an old bed in a country town
carved behind a rail I found these words:
> *Sweet frame and feather*
> *that bore my mother*
> *who bore me who now bear*
> *my long lover*
> *who does me cover*
> *cover him long in care*
We rent these places to play at living
an idyll where we have no living, mimic

belonging here. I have the day to spend
wandering the three streets, wondering
what happened to the woman,
who will have died
generations ago, children
who died or failed or fled the village.
The new young couple came and bought the house
—at what auction, after what disaster?—
to fill a dream, or live in one. Others like us
support the house, the shops on the three streets,

sustained as always by the dream
of money, of exchange and currency.
It circulates the way we do: like blood
descends and thins. It's what we give
and take. It runs
most messages among us.
How should it not be real?
As a teenager I wrote

It is my lot to be
discontented with my lot

with a dull pen inside my closet door
and thought I was unusual.
Evening comes
to the square the church defines. This pump
nostalgic thirst preserved
when water it long drew on drained or went
poisonous with bad rain, and more nostalgia
urged back to work when money came again,
invites me to rest on its stone curb.
I've written off the town. Now I can leave

in my rented car, like one who has eaten
too much confection and declares
he'll fast forever. For a few moments
while night falls I gaze at the fixed linkages
of the pump's skeletal body, scratched by tin cups
and the hoops of buckets, and down at the base
by something sharp, leaving us three letters
and two digits, a person and a date,
even the century hard to guess, a code
nobody living now can break.

SHAVE

I'm thinking about how I shave my face because yesterday
I shaved my father's for the first time. This sun's going to rise
a little farther right now every day. Soon I will return
to my normal life in another city and the year will decay
in an orderly fashion. He gestured me to cut
off the mustache. I wouldn't. Everybody I said, every
damn body should have a mustache. Life *is* trouble.
Later I strode out looking for the car: one who can

walks from the hospital. This mirror,
I can't get it right. The edge of my eye
comes and goes, watering. After a while I know
the days will turn back and walk north. I try to do
what I'm told. My sneeze rings louder in my father's house,
I pace his carpets on naked feet, one of his cigarettes
in my hand. All the machines there hum and glow,
warming up, ready with readouts.

Outside his window, here, a mockingbird
runs on for minutes without repeating, stops
to consider her options, runs it exactly through once more.
She does the wren, the crow, the creaking door.
The sun gives up and lets go of the horizon.
I turn the light off and the razor on,
get back to work on a face I know
even in shadow.

AFTERMATH #87

In the total possession of one idea
such as the idea of a face
so missing it is inescapable

it startles the man in the fast car
on the road taking forever
to wonder why the second cloud from the left

over the mountain so much outreaches
the horn in the belly of cloud below it.
Torn,

he thinks of the incessant history
of waters, those of the sky, those he will call his
until they forgive him by dispersing

as if he sought the blood of angels in a glacier
or probed the fortresses of cells.
On a world near the triple point of water,

where temperature and pressure make the terrible choice
of solid, soft, or invisible
so close to chance it is surely

halfway to indifference,
where could he find
a resting place before the place

where the road ends in the sky?
The mountains. The bones below the eyes.
The scores of rivulets. The snow.

COMMON PRAYER

for Don Bialostosky

I

Training for death you dreamed it every night
how the needle, nicking your hand that held her down
and stroked her, put you to sleep.

An evening by the fire,
over a drink we weigh your dream—
not guilt, pity with complications, but
good simple terror: our dogs
ourselves, like friends or tragic heroes.
I quote your Plato back
"Everything that deceives
may be said to enchant"
in a twisting tone, I grant

Just beyond hearing
like a loaf of charcoal touched with a stick

falling from shape to ash
To look for the lost

Your children made their accommodations:
your daughter who invented
the world's religions one by one
writing the dog letters, drawing her picture
bringing her friends in, toward the end
till you put your foot down
pulling hairs as relics. Your son
adding this to the list
of evidence against the troll
who claims the bridge
and lets us pass
one way

    II
In a kitchen in the past
turn on the light, wash out
a coffee cup, put on water,
measure, begin again.
To look for the lost
find the half-lost and enlist them

as in a forest fire, as out of
pity, as if a talisman against
enchantments that deceive. As
for enchantments that do not
deceive: in the obscure wood
of this long night, light

is that sink's flurorescence
or will-o-the-wisp, or dawn
a small fire between trees.
But as they said, those past
presences who haunt me as I haunt
this house, Stay still

it will come to you. I think
it has come, hardly noticed,
and gone again, again and again,
a little bird the Romans called
passer, always the representative
of the least.

When this body comes to grief
like every body, its pain habitual, a dark suit
worn thin, toward pallor, ghostliness, a ghost
among these rooms I'll move
the way I move now drifting
in the past, among

absences with names.
She can't see me, but the dog
who wanders disspiritedly
into the kitchen looking for dry food
at three in the morning, hours
to go till things get lively

carries half a billion seconds
a hundred trillion miles of time
on her yellow back.
Before I remember I lean down
to touch her, maybe to comb out
a few long hairs with my fingers.

Time for a drink. Would I hurt time
if I could? not passing so much as edging past me
as if I were the dangerous animal, and perhaps
I am. Kill it slowly? If this were now
I could think: if I were gone, what grief
would replace me throughout these rooms?

III

That was the dream that woke me:
On the Arctic shore a male
narwhal: one tooth a clockwise spiral
grown a man's length beyond his lip:
one inside, body heat, falling.

IV

On trips my father drove, my mother played
Twenty Questions with me. Thoughtfully
she would be highway sign or field or car
and dread my turn, always another kind
of whale: Humpback or Right, Cuvier's, True Beaked,
orca or porpoise, Finback, White, Gray, Blue
for miles. My father slept, she drove, I talked
on to the dog, who loved
all traveling but the Pennsylvania
Turnpike tunnels I delighted in.
She hung her yellow face out mile by mile
to slaver in the wind and smell the cows
and turned to lick my face
whenever my talk trailed off, my travelogue
of whales that stayed stern hours out of air
and shifted tons of water with their tails
and could not close their tiny, wrinkled eyes.

V

Four o'clock. Even the birds are still
nestling, cars
at the bottom of the hill let up at last.
I fill
a glass with gin and lime juice by moonlight,
eyes full
with moonlight, my nose and throat fill up
with night
air at last. Lord of my own back yard. A sad dog
bays up,

cuts off short, somewhere behind the lines—pines
that brook
only the least of east light where the dawn
will stream
glory on not through them, where the moon till now
harbored her dim
cargo of pocked blue things. Strewn out around me,
flotsam, these
shadows and makers of shadows seem motionless
ebbing too slowly
to see. They make me itch. It's cold. Maybe it's the gin.
My eyes water.
For all I can do they fill with all they see, half-see,
as in the sea
the mountainous valleyed songs of the whales
sound.

    VI

Maybe at the age of four
I threw the dog out the car window.
My father drove the endless Texas road,
dog and child in the back, till he looked
and the dog was gone. He thought the damn
dog a mess on the asphalt, the child
a trauma, late wherever we were going.

That was the Plymouth, '49 like me,
round-nosed as a baleen, maroon, we painted black
to give it another year or two,
a summer of sandpaper, the three of us by turns
while the dog watched, scratch by scratch,
the wet bright steel burn through.

In the car with both my parents, the dog
beside me, a box of toys, I tired of my book
an Old Mother West Wind by the green cover
and dropped it, with the same preoccupation

that makes me search the freezer for my drink,
out the window. Maybe that was the dog.
When he turned the car around
there on the road she stood
barking to raise the dead.

VII

fulfilled   flag up another day born dead sportive
remonstrous tails slap and tickle needling calling
up so late blowholes on the horn so
rude so Doctor I just can't   sleep and can you do
something about it   yes my child
sit in this chair and hold this pencil tight
write me a story   call it Dream   call it
Whale of a Wish   I will tell you your heart
its deepest fume   o taj mahal   my pet my
self we will go to the seaside   with a pale
and wand   a sceptre scimitar   a sign   please
do not feed the fish   it is written   but
a whale's enamel   grow fingernails again
in direst crisis   conversation   tap out
avoid   avoid   as one of Hamlet's pals
is said to have said   oh   make me dead
good Doctor   make my head   me good   analysis
terminal and in terminals   endless
departures   we promised us
a history and I will have it   take this
train   take this train and hold it
tight   write me a tract   a rite
of way   make way   for whales Doctor at last
I see   concede   I want a whale
joined by God   that we may be one fish
it is better to bury than to mourn

up comes   through desecrations of the royal
pressure   through feat suburbs of plankton
through the looking glass of surface   through
air at last   a big damn shape   Look out

So we might come out into a dream, shared and so true,
true enough, undeceptive, such as would make us
half-lost at most: the fire pleasing, even graceful
for a yellow animal. They eat wood, you know.
That was long before this dawn, before
the moon rose like a pregnant orphan and singled me out,
before I learned remembering resembled being dead, and so on.

Thousands of miles divide us
from where we were friends, hundreds divide us.
We visit. Your dog is dead,
mine's dead as ever. My mother
hollowed and faded out, astounding me. My father died,
friends died. You live, I live,
your wife, your parents, your son and daughter,
her husband, my son, his mother,
and on through our billions plaguing earth.

That night you called
to say how with a preacher's help
you dug the grave for a half-term
damaged child. Later I stood
at the edge and looked to where the park
went black, the nonce pond
glimmered and the stark uneasy
quack of the mother duck in springtime
echoed, wandering
the corridors of dark water
and heard myself call out Take care
little duck
duck, little duck, take care

IX

When the knife goes in it feels good, alarming
but right, alarming because the grain may carry away

too much of the wood, good
because of the smoothness of the grain and the keen blade.

Scoring a line and shaving toward the line,
discovering a tail, making an ear appear,
raising a brown slow drift on the floor all around, a mountain—
this is how the pyramids'

interior decorators made to accompany dead masters on a long
journey much they would need. Wives and friends
servants and armchairs on the walls and beside the pillow
a small dog to stand guard. Over the face a wooden face.

Scoring a line and shaving toward it, I fear
the grain itself drawing this knife too deep.
I pause and my foot stirs
brown dust, my thumb
tests the tree's flesh.

     x

When you held her down lightly on the table
she was quiet like a foal or the mare who bears it.
The doctor filled his hypo with anesthetic
found a vein in the paw and slipped it in
let out a little blood to make sure
of the vein so it swirled cloudily a moment
mixed into anesthetic, and drove it home.
Your hands were still on her head, her shoulder.

I think you saw everything you were doing
like a birthing mare, like time, like an old man
who splits wood to the quarter-inch you want
and knows which way the tree will fall, will fall.
He spits on both his hands before he starts
like time, like any father. Like a foal.

JOINERY

I remember sweating over this
headboard of ours, that

first August, devoting all
my small skill to it

—fitting and making smooth,
planing and, where the plan

ran off in the wild wood,
improvising. I got it

as right as I could get it, love,
not knowing. Over years I learned

not to see it, sleeping there,
night after night, the way we do.

Under its polyurethane
clear coats, slower

than rivers carve or hair grows
grayer, it darkened

to a shape I woke to
just this August morning, more

lovely than any work
I ever intended.

THE THEORY OF SUNDAY

Fog even here, halfway up the hills—
the peaks must make a bowl that wants to brim.
Such radiance stars what's close, including cloud:
a gradient of warmth rendered in water
fine enough to hover and cover everything,
the way a good sleep after too little too long

leaves us groggy. Landmarks like tomorrow,
Veterans' Day and next year will emerge
by afternoon, admonishing; all morning

we stay glad, amid our discrete tasks,
to brush each other in passing like fed cats,
exchanging each time our jot of electricity.

Nor are we living in the past, although
our history of nights like the one just passing
(still passing, the way sounds keep ringing,

like last night's singing, sounds that reach
articulation only as the name
of God, that urged the bed on like an elephant,

and once so alarmed a neighbor she telephoned)
has placed us here, inside this particular cloud.
Instead—I've wanted to tell you though I know

you know, to tell you I know—the morning is
delineation of a field of force
by words fit a few at a time into silence

that hang like a bright cumulus of oil
droplets between charged bodies to demonstrate
the charge, and measure it, if we want to measure it.

Things Coming Toward Their Shadows

mostly falling
speak to us of falling
leaf
I think this through
and my steps begin to meet
the ground like mild ghosts

a monarch
half asleep with autumn
wobbling near my hand
huge wings shuddering
the body back and forth in
pendulous air

in heedless election
falls and clings
to the base of my thumb
ebony pipestem
legs embrace
the feet prickle

the tongue
hangs like a mainspring
O for the moment I
bear that weight
I weigh
nothing else

from Except to Be

Anatomy

Over three-quarters of a year two people can make the entire anatomy of a third; once physiology has ceased, the ground and its inhabitants unmake an anatomy in a few years. Sitting with my chin on my curled knuckles and my elbow on my knee, I marvel again at "the nonce anatomy of lap and fist." Here I have two *things*—my fist; my lap—I can make appear and disappear from the world in an instant.

Does this miracle depend on language? I put one hand on my hip, and I make a shape. However distinctive, it has no name (no noun, though we might dredge up the adjective "akimbo"). But it constitutes a *thing* as much as do the reified gestures of closed hand and bent legs. Yet given this pair, "fist" and "lap," by the language, we can construct a whole human range: the poles of rage and comfort; declarations of intent to move (a fist wants to strike out) and intent not to move (I shall sit down).

One *can* make fists with one's toes, and a lap of sorts with one's arms—for a cat, perhaps.

ANTS

Spend half an hour watching ant trails. You can tell that they don't in our way follow each other; their feeler-greetings (so quick it takes long minutes to convince oneself that they do greet, rather than simply bumping into each other) argue intuitively against their having very good eyesight. They follow trails of scent or taste (our separate names for gaseous and liquid chemical messages, due to our so queerly having separate orifices for the two).

After a time it becomes clear that some ants follow these trails more efficiently than others: Coming upon a bump in the brick, one out of ten or twenty will wander around the "wrong" (unmarked) side—obviously a loser, though nearly all find their way back eventually. (They use the Monte Carlo or "drunkard's walk" algorithm, beloved of programmers specializing in computer simulations of systems such as ant colonies.) Just as clearly, only these bumblers can bear any credit for new trails. The good soldiers never deviate and never discover. The colony owes its life in the short run to the good citizens; in the long run, since no single source of food lasts forever, it relies on the mavericks. As Shaw reminds us: "The reasonable man adapts himself to the world: the unreasonable one persists in trying to adapt the world to himself. Therefore all progress depends on the unreasonable man."

BRICK

In French, the object (*une brique*) precedes the substance (*le brique*); English reverses this word-history no doubt by simple accident. Perhaps again by accident the compound "bryke wallis" (later "brickwalls") arrives into

English first (1440). *Brick* served also as plural. The word stems (Teutonic to French to English) from *brek-an*: the brick as broken-off piece, originally of bread, which later came in loaves called "bricks" from their resemblance to the building brick: an exchange of similarities. By 1527 the object had so established itself that we specified its broken pieces as *brykendis*.

The first mortar after mud (Ur, 4000 BC, an arch now fallen) we made from bitumen slime.

Though Augustus boasted of having found his capital brick but left it marble (Gibbon, 1776), London after the Great Fire of 1627 embraced brick with all its heart. *A brick* signified praise among Victorians for whom the virtue of solid dependability held little irony. Coming down on someone *like a thousand of brick* (or *a ton of bricks*) displayed the strength of righteous anger. America had mixed feelings: In conversation during the twenties one avoided *dropping a brick*, and someone drunk in the late nineteenth century *wore a brick in his hat*.

Modern bricks come in various sizes (most often 8" x $3^3/_4$" x $2^1/_4$"), but in 1724 the Tilers' and Bricklayers' ordinances set them at 9 by $4^1/_2$ by $2^1/_4$ inches. Yet the symmetry, each side half the last, merely decorated the profound requirement that a brick fit the bricklayer's hand, whose other held the trowel to mortar and tap it into place.

Ask people to name "a thing" and, after tables, bricks come most often to mind: perfect uniform solidity, perfectly comprehensible by both the eye and the imagination of the hand.

For the University of Virginia campus he designed, Jefferson invented the serpentine wall: longer than a straight one, but stable though only one brick thick, and so more efficient of bricks, overall, in the labor-poor new country.

GLASS

New glass has a tensile strength five times the best practical steel, and twice the theoretical limit of steel. Glass weakens, both through fatigue and through chemical action ("poor resistance to attack by alkaline solutions. Thus, the familiar soda-lime glass contains the agent of its eventual destruction" [*Encyclopedia Britannica XI*]).

The favorite fact about glass: A liquid, it flows ("glacially") downward, producing ripples and, eventually, a thickness at the bottom perhaps twice that of the top. The difference in time-scale of this flow, from the speed of light on the one hand, and from the duration of human habitations on the other, renders glass useful for windows.

Sound-effects specialists, who make thunder from hammered tin and decanting wine from the rapid popping of tongue against palate, imitate breaking glass by breaking glass, in a box or bag for neatness.

Hermit Thrush

perhaps five hundred times in a summer's day, the main theme often followed by a B-minor triad and variations falling by whole steps. Of course the bird sings something quite different; not only does it include trills and mordents and *ports de voix* too fast and high for human ears (for which the bird does not intend them) but the whole fiction of time- and key-signatures belongs to a system of notation by which the singer does not feel bound. His art (the male sings) eschews the well-tempered octave, and of course we would err in calling it art. Yet can anyone believe that the blunt force of species self-identification for purposes of territorial announcement and mating invitations governs his every choice of variation, minute by minute? Should we call the variation *error*?

Theodore Roosevelt could find "nothing in the Nightingale's song to compare" with "the serene, ethereal beauty of the Hermit's song." *Et tu, Europa.*

Khoof

The first revolution in dining technology since the 15th-century advent of the fork will overtake us shortly with the introduction of the khoof.

Made usually of finely machined lightweight ceramic, the khoof consists of a kind of tined spoon with a retractable finger covering the bowl. The mechanism of the best khoofs retracts the finger in a shallow cycloidal arc, though cruder rectilinear designs lower the price.

Its main uses include otherwise unmanageable foods such as rice, dry cereals, trail mix, and stir-fry. One can properly eat peas with the khoof. In place settings, the khoof goes between the knife and the spoon, despite the resulting increase in unbalance.

It shares with spoon and fork a symmetry that renders right- and left-handed khoofs unnecessary.

LUSTRON

The housing shortage after World War II found one solution in the Lustron house. Metal panels with enamel paint baked on, shipped to the building site on a flatbed, bolted together, the seams sealed with rubber gaskets, formed an outer wall (the panels large and square, like the shells of many gas stations since) and an inner wall (room-tall panels with shallow vertical grooves to remind us of boards), with warm air pumped between the two for comfort. For floors, one-foot-square asphalt tiles covered a simple cement slab. Interior doors slid open and closed with a friendly, hollow rumble. (Caitlin remarks: "Like living on the Starship *Enterprise*.") To hang posters and photographs on the walls, one used small magnets.

The houses went up so quickly and therefore cheaply that only a few thousand appeared before the building-trades unions quashed the whole movement.

In the St. Louis winter mornings, my mother would come out of my parents' bedroom in her nightgown, turn up the heat, and lean against the wall as it warmed.

MACADAMIZED

Stylists sometimes object to hybrid words ("interloper" mixes Latin and Dutch) but who can fail to admire "macadamized," with its four root languages? The surname of the road-building inventor, John Loudon McAdam, domesticates Hebrew (Adam) with a Gaelic prefix; his process adds the French operative suffix "-ise"; and the sign of the participle, "-ed," carries over from Anglo-Saxon.

Tar-macadam, or "tarmac," improved on the original layers-of-gravel design early in this century.

When Victoria visited the redesigned Paris in 1855 she approved how Louis-Napoleon had macadamized his streets "to prevent the people from taking up the pavement [blocks] as hitherto"—not for building or for pranks, but for flinging at police. *Britannica XI* notes that the city's new design replaced tired Renaissance imitations with a "rational" architecture "taking full account of practical wants." It does not mention that the wants belonged primarily to the military category. Haussmann, the designer, made wide boulevards, to transport riot-breakers quickly from one end of the city to the other; long straight streets, to provide clear fields of fire; with graceful oblique intersections, to afford troops some surprise in outflanking barricades.

Racket

No one blind could play squash, despite *Tommy*. Yet a deaf squash player labors under an unappreciated disadvantage. The player who turns to watch how her opponent shoots may get a face sufficiently full of squash ball (average speed in tournament play, 135 m.p.h.). Instead, she hears how hard the other's racquet hit the ball, and whether square in the sweet spot or, perhaps, deceptively hard off a bit of the racquet's frame. None of this communicates direction, but may dictate whether she needs a quick run to the front court or a judicious retreat toward the back wall.

Blow-Up ends with a tennis match the photographer watches intently, as we watch his face; but our ears—and his? who can know?—receive the exchanged shots made in fact by two mimes with imaginary racquets and an imaginary ball.

The squash player hears not volume so much as pitch and timbre.

Seventy-Eights

A man who left St. Louis in 1961 could not transport his eleven hundred immaculate jazz seventy-eight-r.p.m. records: fragile ten-inch disks weighing perhaps half a pound each. He advertised; my father answered; and since we too planned to move in the Fall, he borrowed a tape recorder from some acquaintance in the audio-visual business: therefore a professional machine; therefore, in those days, a monster packed into two footlockers, which took over the dining room. All summer each family member must on entering the house record at least one (1) disk, loading a new seven-inch reel of tape as necessary, and noting all contents of the disk's label on a master list. We got nearly half of them done: excellent copies of Billie Holiday, Coleman Hawkins, Count Basie, Chu Berry, and so on, years before the record companies began their reissue programs.

Later my father found occasional seventy-eights of interest, which led him to locate old seventy-eight-r.p.m. turntables, already becoming rare, and rebuild them.

The interest of some seventy-eights lay, more intrinsically, in the aluminum disk inside the layers of vinyl when that material replaced the brittle bakelite, taking the groove of music better but at first incapable of supporting its own weight. Sheet aluminum, splendid for building small boxes for electronic components, cost more per square foot than old records. So I remember my father boiling batches of them in a big kitchen pot to peel away the sound-bearing black plastic.

Sirens

In the popular image, three sirens sing to lure sailors to shipwreck: death by distraction. Homer indicates only two, whom he neither names nor describes. Later we hear of three, named Parthenope, Ligea (yes, Poe), and Leucosia, and see them as birds with women's faces or women with wings, not wholly distinct from the Eumenides or harpies. But "later writers" (Apollodorus in particular) also give two of them a lyre and a flute (as if the flautist could join her sisters in song), making nonsense of Orpheus's rescue of the Argonauts by drowning out their singing with his lyre—the first skirmish in the long war between vocal and instrumental music. We learn of their island, Anthemoëssa, off Italy, and of their parentage in a river god and one or another of the Muses (most often Melpomene, the one in charge of tragedy).

As far as Homer could tell, or others after him, the desire to destroy sailors provided the sirens' whole motive. Fanciful commentators took this ball and ran with it, decreeing that the sirens would die if anyone passed unharmed. (Parthenope, washed up after Odysseus sneaked by, gave her name to the first city on the site of Naples.) But the literature makes it clear that the victims died not on their rocks, but of hunger from lingering to listen. Does overpowering beauty plausibly derive from spite? The sirens desire to sing. If they sing to sailors, they sing to please them; the pleasure creates the danger, rather than serving as the instrument of the danger. The implications for sexual politics—sirens have always filled a mythic role—shine out clearly.

In the New World, later sailors saw manatees and cried, "Sirenes!" Zoologists still call their order *sirenia*.

TAPIR

When I visited the tapir in the San Francisco zoo—feeling melancholy, and leaving my friends to the birds and monkeys—one of their number came to the fence and consented to my scratching it on its side, at the shoulder. As I scratched it leaned against the fence and closed its eyes. When I stopped, it straightened onto its tapered legs and unmistakably *glared* at me, wrinkling its astonishing proboscis. I returned to my task of scratching and it to its leaning. When at last I took my hand away, I found it wet and covered with quarter-inch-long dark-olive hairs, and it smelled sweet, like a day-old salad.

Kubrick uses tapirs in *2001* to represent the animals beside which the ape-men graze, and which become their first prey after the Monolith starts the civilization game.

Huxley: "One taper burns, but 'tis too much . . . "

TELEVISIONS

Even dead they cause problems. The tube, the most ubiquitous vacuum in American homes, can implode violently when cracked. As a child I puzzled over this threat, this danger posed by *nothing*, until I learned to apply the principles of kinetic energy: Glass fragments, having rushed suddenly inward, can't simply stick in the center, but must bounce forcefully out, showering the careless.

I recall two of my father's projects to neutralize defunct televisions. One: He lays the machine on its face on the garage floor with the tail of the tube sticking a few inches above the wooden case, he slings a rope over a beam directly above it, ties a hammer to the end, holds the long end of the rope, and directs me to swing the hammer (from a safe distance) at the target; after half a dozen tries we hear the satisfying pop and tinkle, then dump out the glass crumbs, so well contained by the case. Two: He puts the old tube in the new tube's shipping carton, goes two doors down the suburban street to get (as a fellow veteran, I think) permission from the local sheriff, sends me inside to watch longingly, stands the box in the yard against the garage wall, and (in his overcoat and galoshes) aims a .22 rifle at the condemned; one shot does it.

Year: 1250

David de Stockton (my first known ancestor), *floruit* at the time of the great British Schoolmen—Roger Bacon, Alexander of Hales, William of Occam, Duns Scotus, and on the continent Albertus Magnus and Thomas Aquinas— under the reign of Henry III, who succeeded bad old King John in 1216. (Did de Stockton's birth coincide with the death of Robin Hood?) Newish words in English included *anger, annoy, appear* (of angels, etc.), *arithmetic, bedtime, bigamy, bush, butler* . . . Already the Norman aristocracy taught their children French as a foreign language.

Knitting may have reached England from Scandinavia. The longbow, just introduced from Wales, started the knights' escalation of fashion from mail to plate armor. Treadles previously used for looms began to power lathes. Half a century before, navigators first used the compass, England got its earliest windmills, and water-driven fulling mills initiated the English dominance in textiles. The cathedral at Chartres, begun during Richard's reign before John's usurpation, neared completion.

Another fifty years would introduce clocks, and paper, and Marco Polo's *Travels*, and the spinning wheel. (In 1250 women span with spindle and whorl, a meter at a time—a slow method, but portable. The wheel would bind them to the cottage.)

Elsewhere, Koreans began using movable type (200 years before Guttenburg's reinvention), Amazonian Indians (not "Indians" for another 242 years) used rubber to waterproof their clothes, and others may have experimented with the hot-air balloon.

Year: 1949

Words new to print in English in the year of my birth: avionics, banalize, Big Brother, cortisone, daddy-o, desalinate, dexamphetamine, dolorimeter, doublethink, Dramamine, drive-through, Emmy, Fair Deal, fluoridate, hologram, home perm, instantiation, Isolette, kibutznik, Knesset, launderette, matrilineage, methamphetamine, micrometeorite, mid-range, Monte Carlo (mathematics), neomycin, newspeak, nosecone, obsessively, patrilineage, p-n-p (transistors), polymorphously, post-modern, pseudologue, pseudorandom, purportedly, quiche, rheumatology, Ritalin, scripted, self-fulfilling, shtetl, slimline, sparagmos, staffer, supercalifragilisticexpialidocious, taco, telethon, Tex-Mex, ultrathin, unperson, video recording, Wild Turkey, zonk, and Zydeco.

Russian Lessons

for Helen Reeve

I. Words and Things

Sergei Mikhailovich my greeter and first guide
walks me all over Red Square declaiming
that no nation should be run from a cemetery.
I ask the name of the little bird before us.
Tryasaguzka, he says, and gropes:
"Tryasa, shake; and guzka, how do you say,
ass." He demonstrates.
Ah. Wagtail.

II. Shopping

I've learned enough about Moscow lines
to join one in the street: something essential
has just turned up. Light bulbs. Slowly I realize
the bulbs are all dead. You take the dead bulb
to your office and switch it for a live one
which you take home. The office
might be able to get new bulbs
and if not, who needs to see at work?

III. Kopeck

At the official rate the fifteen-kopeck coin
was about a dime. Now the fall
of the ruble from one and a half per dollar
to a thousand or fifteen hundred
has driven the incalculable
kopeck from circulation. Kiosks
following the steely law of markets
peddle the coins, which are still
all the pay phones will take, for
sixty-seven times face value:
about a penny.

IV. PUBLIC ENTRANCE

Misha and Ksusha won't hear of my going
alone to the Hermitage and paying four, five
tourist dollars. Russians get in for ten
or twenty rubles. "We pay enough taxes for it,"
they will smuggle me in through a friend.
When Misha (artist) went to London
and rushed to the Royal Gallery
and asked a guard where to buy a ticket, the guard
pointed glacially at the name carved over the door:
"Do you know what *Royal* means?"

V. COMMERCE

Three militsia in gray greatcoats,
tall and thin and as always very young,
hang around a street-vendor's place,
empty, a scale. As they all smile
and wait for whatever is going to happen,
one of them is weighing his handcuffs.

VI. INSTRUCTION

It is important to learn the words
for numbers. In the store you must find out
the price, which may not be written
on a sign. Go and tell it to the cashier.
Beside the cash register sits a humpbacked abacus.
Do not hand your money to the cashier
but place it on the little plate before her
on the counter. She will replace it
with your change and receipt. Take the receipt
back to the sales desk, and exchange it
for your bread. Twenty-seven rubles. Two cents.

VII. DACHA

During our weekend I learn that all this settlement
is retired generals and colonels. Kamal tells me
the word for *frog* in his Dhagestani. The sound,

very like a frog, defies
the letters known to English.
Kyra sings and weeds.
While we sit on a pile of warm logs, the luminous-
eyed Anya, neighbor, seventeen, asks
to read my poems, offering in exchange
her prized volumes: Hesse, or
Jim Morrison's lyrics. Little Artur
names the Ninja Turtles on his t-shirt
the Renaissance reborn in a New York sewer
and shows me his toy cars: "I also have
a pick-up truck, an Alfa Romeo, and a Ferrari."

VIII. PETER'S BURG
The beauty of the city
has seven reasons. It was caused
to be built (1) all at once at (2)
a perfect Wedgwood moment of European style
by someone who had plentiful (3) money
and (4) expendable workers, and who made
two laws: that (5) no building could exceed
the stories of the long low Winter Palace now
Hermitage and (6) none could be any
taller than the street in front was wide. You could
lay them flat on their faces. (7) Rivers, canals.
Forty-two islands.

IX. ROBOT, FROM *RABOTYET,* IT WORKS
In the Moscow office I type a letter
on the computer of my host's secretary,
who will fax it home for me. She prints it
using two sheets and the first
carbon paper I have seen in a decade,
since ribbons are not obtainable.

X. THINGS AND WORDS

Viktor cuts an herb into our soup. No cook,
I ask him, "What is this herb?" He tells me
in Russian, pauses, knife wavering.
Translating has never given him
the need for the English. Literary,
we leave the broth to cool
and go to his study to look it up.
The dictionary says: "chervil;
dill." But chervil
is not dill, I say.
We sit down to eat, baffled.

XI. NATURAL ASSUMPTION

One day in the cafeteria I panic
to see the cashier using the abacus,
not the register which shows the price
in perspicuous Arabic, but is on the blink.
But the amount she rattles off is
trista tritye tri
which I understand. She wants smaller change
than my four hundred rubles. I pull out my wad
of tiny tens and ones and sort them. She helps with this,
as if my incompetence
extended to the numbers on the bills.

XII. SECURITY

In the middle of the department store
a smoked-glass building-within-a-building
offers a Jeep Grand Cherokee
for fifty million rubles, or about two hundred
and thirty-one years of Russian salary.
Big men stand in the cool shadows.

XIII. SIGNS

In the Scholars' Club, Lev and I drink beer.
He pulls out a cigarette. Conscientious

in my smidge of Russian, I mention
a sign over the bar I am sure declares
No Smoking. Without turning, Lev
counsels: you don't see it. If the proprietor comes
you apologize for not seeing it. Meanwhile
hold your cigarette more or less under the table.

xiv. Woes

In Misha's kitchen we discuss American aid.
Dubious, he tells me the old story:
a fellow passing by a swamp
sees a man plunged deep in it.
"I'm coming!" he cries, and with great labor
hauls him to dry land. On the road, the man says,
"Why did you pull me out? I live there."

xv. Russia

In the path near my dormitory
thickly overgrown with ragged bushes
a slim tree forcing through asphalt
extends along the ground
at a slope of less than thirty degrees
for more than ten meters
before it finds daylight and puts forth
its bushy prize of leaves.

Saints

A squirrel more worried
by winter's approach than mine
eats fast, not neatly, eight feet away.
If she's not a saint
she needs one.

If a glory didn't have
a hole in it we'd never know.

The rent lets us in
to look around, lets the saint out,
where the heaven spills

to give us all this blue.
Aren't we all holy? Are they here
or there? Do we care
how they died, or die?
Do we even want them

to neglect themselves,
or only to connect
with home? Their place or ours?
A church is what makes rules for saints.
Is it true

that when they walk they leave
a trail of golden feathers
& the odd iron-bound book,
th'angelic Number One & Number Two?
No, that is a lie.

Is my dog allowed? She expired
long ago, which is I know required.
She never bit a god. The hair around her head
stood out in a great rrruff
any painter would do in gold.

THE MASQUE OF MEASURE

WHY I BEGAN YOUR STORY
Some drivers worry all the time. Precautions must be exercised in the handling of plutonium to avoid unintentional formation of a critical mass. Sometimes in fall we hear geese crossing the night sky, blind. You can tell how the sheet goes by how the flowers go. During a 3-month period 6 in 10 adults reported purchasing at least 1 book. Nevertheless' biological differences do

exist between groups of men, as we all know.

The medley is one of the minor arts. Cover each layer with a rack, invert, remove the pan, peel off the paper lining, cover with another rack and invert again, leaving the layer right side up to cool. Even before birth our destinies were tied together. The silk flowers are thick with dust. We ease into each other, while too many cooks mill around downstairs. Weasel brains. Metamorphosis usually accompanies change of habits or of habitat.

THE EROTICS OF PARENTHESIS

These are predacious fishes, chiefly tropical. The American Forestry Association publishes a Social Register of Big Trees. Absent Pauli's exclusion principle, there would be one electron in the whole universe. While Heraclitus cannot be thinking of Mandelbrot, Mandelbrot can be thinking of Zeno.

Love forty. The highroads are dreary but they lead to the town. Two particles exert a mutual force by exchanging a third particle. Up yours too. For most organisms three billion years ago oxygen was a deadly poison. When the wind blows, the tree shakes. This World Series really cuts into your off-season. Only Pennsylvania and Mississippi have produced Miss Americas in successive years. We must hasten, as the darkness is increasing very rapidly.

The element is available to qualified purchasers from the Nuclear Regulatory Commission at a price in the range of $1,000/gram (80-99% enriched). Daniell Abbot then Chosen Constable but Possitive Refvsed to accept it; whereupon Zachary Jones was Chosen Constable. It happened about nine thousand days ago. My image of your vagina isn't visual but kinesthetic. To leave out of consideration all the other things, the immortal gods have so aided us that nothing seems to have been neglected.

HISTORY

I quit work and went to bed. That is:

I saved my file, shut down the computer and switched off the lamp over my desk. I went to the bedroom, undressed, and lay down to sleep. That is:

I stood up from my desk chair in the dark, moved toward the door whose position lay fixed in memory, walked down hall/stairs/hall to the first and last door of the day, opened and entered it. I found and freed the buttons of my shirt, pushed shoes and socks off feet and into their grumbling corner, peeled away jeans and underwear, and donned a loose singlet of blue emblazoned "Trinidad" where I had never been. Turning to the bed, turning back the sheet, I turned in place and sitting fell to my side, turning in toward sleep beside you. That is

another story.

JUST SUPPOSE

Only anxious people create musical works, and only composers write many letters. Some drivers dwell in California. Only Republicans compose few letters. Animals besides hippos don't drive cars. No Californians don't pen poems. No anxious people are hippopotami. In short, some poets are Republicans.

THE NEPHEWS OF ROMULUS

The argument, to be sure, is a good one. Think of the White House: a summit not high, but steep. No finite source of radiation is a true point, but any source viewed from a sufficient distance may be considered as a point source.

Light, and not the lake, moves through the sycamores. When I think of your body I get cotton and otters. We heard that the general was drawing up his troops in that place. "Plaisir d'amour" interrupts a "train" of thought.

You can tell if a politician is lying, said the comedian, by whether his lips are moving. *Glubit* is used by Cato of stripping the bark off an oak, by Varro of skinning sheep, by Catullus (#58) of Lesbia in the alley with her *magnanimi Remi nepotes*. Half a moment. To obtain the latex, which does not flow readily from living trees, the tree may be felled and a series of rings cut in the bark. To the shepherd, all is flocks.

I am dying, Egypt. This chair hasn't been moved in years.

ASSEZ SOIGNÉE

A herd can hardly be said to age. He that for every little occasion is moved with compassion, is called piteous, which is a sickness of the mind, wherewith at this day the more part of men be diseased.

"The Romans did not practice circumcision" is a pentameter. Slide over a little. Under your clothes your weight shifts lightly.

The earth, of course, is spherical only to a first approximation. I think I would do anything for you. Come, come. The Amendment limiting a President's terms of office was ratified a month after Eisenhower's inauguration. There was no one but saw him and heard all he said. Baudelaire was not from St. Louis. This ethnic group should not be confused with the viol of the same name. The tops of the rows of pines are all equal; the tops of the pines are equal. I am doing a great work so that I cannot come down. *Reader's Digest* was founded the year "The Waste Land" was published.

Per capita, twice as many white Americans as black Americans, and three times as many men as women, commit suicide. I do not know that anyone has written a satisfactory history of cruelty, though certain special aspects of it, such as torture, have been studied. Behold, a scene nearly as bare as its words. In memory not yet green.

LANGUE ON PAROLE

Amy eats complexity. These replicas are for Brian, whose aptitudes and appetites were never in doubt. Carmen calls to mind long strokes of an oar. With the run of the mill it's six of one half dozen of the other, but as God is my witness once he gets on his high horse there's no stopping Derek. Listen to Elissa, listing eels. For Ferdinand, everything in the newspapers—constabulary pronouncements, classified desire, the whole bilge bulge—lacks the requisite flair. Gertrude's a hurricane. Hazael appears to have proved what the prophet foresaw him to be, a man of violence, cruelty and blood. A sole I sold Isolde is old. Up, John. I'll take you home *again*, Kathleen. Hats off to Larry. Hail, Mary, full of grace and charm.

When I remember Nathan, I think of the way young birds at the moment spring runs over into summer shift from foot to foot and are gone before you can blink. And Olga, fifteen. At Herodia's behest, Salome requests the head from Herod's brother, her father the tetrarch of Itrurea—that's Philip. Queenie who disobeys, me disobeys. Ralph doesn't have to see the sun to know it's there. We have to thank Sabrina, since we have her to thank. When Tom remarked that his name backwards was the French word for *word* we were speechless. Foremost among those who believe in art for art's sake, Ursula feels she owes her very presence to that vital principle. On the next page Vladimir dies shamefully. While what we'd wanted was waning, we were wondering where Wanda went. About Xuthus, son of Hellen, no one has cared. You take Yolanda there. The verb is "to father," as Zachary fathered the Baptist heretic.

As We Get Closer and Closer to the Winter Solstice
We'll See More and More of This Kind of Weather

An interlocutor is virtually essential: it is hard to talk to yourself for hours on end. Heraclitus is said instead of publishing his treatise, which survives in brief but numerous fragments, to have deposited it in the temple of Artemis. Ezra Pound's first book appeared in the year of invention of the silencer. The highest functions of the brain, judgment and insight, are the last to return after coma. Viz., we fucked until daylight. He heard himself use the exorbitant word, the very sound of which helped to determine his flight.

The United States opposes changing international law to raise the universal combat age from 15 to 18. You take route 3 from Choluteca across the border, then 24 and 12 into Managua. The water will be too cold for bathing. I am poured out like water, and all my bones are out of joint. Chitin is chemically extraordinarily inactive. The root of *waltz* and *walk* and *welter* is also the root of *vulva, helix,* and *gabardine.* That boy said that that that that that girl parsed was not that that that that gentleman meant. The (computer) sex (bulletin) boards are "truly advertising as conversation."

Key to Trees in Leafless Condition

Does the making of a monster sometimes begin from a single decision not to worry so much? Mustn't there be a moment when the one wave after the last to break freezes? Is it sometimes funny when the crisis of one person's life coincides with another's most daily round—suicide and the policeman? Do you have one moment? Can you fiddle down, fiddle down down, fiddle down down, fiddle down? Have you got enough room? If we keep adding more energy, can we keep generating more massive particles? Is this what you wanted?

From a Cambridge roof, did Joe Haldeman watch the occultation of Procyon? Was "Does your chewing gum lose its flavour on the bedpost overnight?" the only American success by a skiffle band? Do my friends have friends named the Hands and the Elbows?

Can we talk?

Is the air of past ages trapped in pockets in the snows of yesteryear? Is your first memory the memory of a smell? Have I already asked this? Do you have the feeling our motions exact the attention of beings millions of parsecs from here? Are we moving as well as you would like?

HONK IF YOU LOVE JESUS

*If you got born again
what sign would you be?*

The updated manual
sleeps beneath the willows of afternoon
which replaced the cool, taller willows of dawn
with a silent flourish, with a stiff spine.

My car needs your car
as you need the manual, as the machine
the manual needs needs you.
The music starts, they all move over one.

Quickly before these daffodils or pinks
can count to ten
consider them.
Any time the light goes wrong

you think you hear your mother calling you.
But when the curled hand bears down on the wheel
and the prairie flowers with red messages—
too late—then pray as I have instructed you.

THE LONG VIEW

Doth not the ear try words?

I

Now for the little ecstasy of things
as they leave the gray mere shaded
landscape, springing

clear to the eye as gist, composed
say of a wildfire strew of stones
in a wedge rising from left to right

gray mortar a ground for white
blue bice russet lavender crowding
faces of protruding stone

I've traded in
the sevenheaded angels of the brain
to look at a wall

a quarter mile off
a whole chorus round or fittingly hewn oblong
and to settle something

for the better in words
or worse
just never to do it again

II
Nothing can be undone
Penelope
you intricate

the act, that's all
however you struggle
by torchlight

to subtract
to perfect
the blank sheet

while the walls around you
record on their endless film
the multiplying layers of your laboring shadow

One of the women
wall-eyed
looked to another

master—"So
against her will and by force she had
to finish it"

III
Orbit (Doctor Gray): to protect
"from injury, whilst its position
is such as to ensure the most extensive

range"—from where else
would we choose to do
our business, our self

-imposed and -satisfied protocols
for coming to resemble certain pots: thick
glaze over a half-baked shape

From here every journey
starts out (while the ear takes in)
toward sky: "Go to"

and they had brick for stone
and slime had they
for morter, for a city and a tower

"And let us make a name" they said
"lest we be scattered abroad
upon the face of the whole earth"

IV
Shuttle: We hear the weaving
was "glorious"
and she

"expert in beautiful work"
but never
what the work was

Scenes of Laertes' life
his son's ramblings
the whole world's favorite war

she strove against
by night
How carefully she applied herself all day

"She is winning"
Antinoös concedes
"a great name for herself"

These isometrics
won three years, when only time
could be won

v

A square
is a square from anywhere
on a line normal to its plane and piercing

the center: that infinity of points
and nowhere else
From anywhere on either plane

including a diagonal
and the center line
except on the line,

a figure like the kite the eye sometimes
attaches to, foreshortened, rising
across blue space far on a hill of wind, tiny

in high summer, the running child out of sight
Elsewhere a trapezoid
Else a box

whose paired sides say by exact convergence
there you are at such an angle
but still *sweet bird* what distance

VI
As Gombrich says
I wouldn't
however unsuperstitious

take a friend's picture
and pin it up
through the eyes

or look in the mirror
into my eye
and say

vile jelly
as in *out*
vile jelly

though all of us stood on the round earth
gazing to where the fire we'd made
pushed the white kite, with high hearts

and everybody looks up and says "Aww!"
but this time
fireworks and a dead end

VII
"A house"
said Steven Ross
"is an instance of a program"

a sequence of computable intentions
made up in stone, ice, paper
a system knit like Fenollosa's world

from simple imperatives:
add this to that
fetch

wait
You could be anywhere
out of the air

So where this glass meets this memory
is *here*
Who

we are is where
we have been
going

VIII
Inside a room, the windowed
dayshine rummages
everywhere—so one

bit (after and altered by
this very expensive photograph
of all of us, at home) homes in

This light
combines colors: excites
the vortices of matter:

has a history of lenses
glass after glass
deflections from surfaces

and through them:
hastens:
may gladden:

vibrates: acts like a motion
and like a moving thing: can lift
(Einstein proved) the latch of a door

IX
Leonardo "cannot forbear to mention
a new device for study which, though it seem
but trivial and almost ludicrous, arouses

the mind to various inventions. And this is,
when you look at a wall spotted with stains,
or with a mixture of stones,

if you have to devise some scene, you may
discover a resemblance
to various landscapes, beautified

with mountains, rivers, rocks, trees, plains,
wide valleys and hills in varied arrangement;
or again you may see battles and figures in action;

or strange faces and costumes, and an endless variety
of objects, which you could reduce
to complete and well drawn forms. And these appear

on such walls confusedly, like the sound of bells
in whose jangle you may find
any name or word you choose to imagine."

X
"The ice
where I stood suddenly
broke into a carpet of hexagonal Venusian flowers

the shoes of the next man flickered
with brandy blue flame
OK

but my friend broke down
into a sequence
of moments that would not stop

being moments or a sequence or add up
so fear so not friend so grab something
so I woke up

in the camp hospital
with those thick white paws
and a kind of discharge

days after the funeral
When I clean houses now
I won't wash windows"

XI
Only the odd brick sticking
across iron rust stippling through leprous
paint in drools a glutinous youth

put out, hardened—a place to wait
for rain to collect dirt
Towers at the corners

at my head and feet dull atmosphere
glare drain dull sound of guards' feet
smudged shrubs considering violence

not a chance
this noctilucent afternoon
to put any best light on it

Carry a telescope a mile away
or a quarter million
and bring this place so close

it could hang back in a new celebrity
priceless
between thumb and index

    XII
One Ford one Mercury etc.
four hills of assorted buildings brick
wood brick brick stone brick wood stone one woman

reading a *National*
Enquirer (Jesus what a great
glass) a group gathered beside a tractor

gulls in a row windows
in phalanx taking the hazy sun
a mass of asphalt waiting to be painted

antenna dishes and antenna trees and one man
hosing off another's boot in the train yard
sprawled skeins of brown track

a man in the parking lot
sucking down a beer
so close

I can almost
taste it, the throat working
working

    XIII
If as it might well
thine eye offend thee
Though thou exalt thyself

as the eagle and though thou set
thy nest among the stars
wandering stars

to whom is reserved
the blackness of darkness for ever
If the mind minds

its situation, little circuit—cast it
cast the damn shuttling yo-yo out
the window mouth gate window pineal

body:
If thine eye offend
close it

"Thus do I save
myself
for death" that bides time

    XIV
Say how Bach
is braided by the open window
with the smell of insecticide

and rain
and how the Bach, the first
movement of the last partita

on a fine if baby
grand piano is badly played and how delicately
by the sweetish smell is childhood evoked

Windows by only being
open become responsible
or closed

as when a woman in her kitchen
back of the big apartment house
was thrown against the wall

imagine her delicate situation
over and over for an hour not seen
unheard

    X V
Donald Menzel:
Look at a bright star
with your naked eye

do not be concerned
if the star appears to possess
a few minute points

most people
have some minor eye imperfections
that add points to the stars

I look at the city
which appears to possess a few minute points
I am not concerned

Then how could it happen
without moving
the light leaps out of things

everywhere, each of the hills is flame
high cloud silvers the brilliant river
the blade of grass unfurls its name

    X V I
George Paulus
in a brick summer school room
before time got its first bad name

said Imagine
that you are an eye
a sphere seeing every direction equally

and your life is rolling
on the surface of an indefinitely large
mirror

That is a use of the imagination
to bring itself to focus
in curved glass

In the math he taught lines always met
Now in a photograph I keep
the round world gazes out of square space

glaucous, pole
cataracted by cloud, the whole
hanging glassed and black framed between windows

XVII
"When my hands, cold and trembling, shall no longer
clasp and against my will
shall let fall

on my bed of suffering" the pen the crucifix
ball of twine book crystal telescope fork
idea groped after in my dotard chat

I want six crap shooters to bear me out
glass of whiskey
at my head and feet

"When my imagination
afflicted with the sight
of my iniquities

and the terror of thy judgments
shall fight the angel
of darkness who conceals thy mercy

from mine eyes
merciful Jesus"
put a jazz band on my hearse to raise hell

XVIII

"The ear that heareth
the reproof of life
abideth among the wise"

The eye
that dwells on it
comes to no good

Zeno was wrong
We get somewhere, say
the embryos:

the eye is where the skin grows in
to meet the brain
again

to focus—the Latin word
for hearth
a mercy at last just

to sort from the mullions and the distance first
the bird a shadow on the hill
and then the bird

from ISLAND

TAMBOURINE

Also, he made a molten sea of ten cubits from
brim to brim, round in compass . . . and a line
of thirty cubits did compass it round about.
          —2 CHRONICLES 4:2

Now:

I walk a coast brilliant as dragon glass
        for water flinging splinters chaotic alongside
                and in the distance long orders of island
                        spun for the occasion out of morning
                                corporeal light

As mythical violence sets a bloodline running
        a cooler intention now
                austerely furnishes the horizon broad O

Light examines me

Isometric leaning wind
        beatifies this mind
                grown credulous as air

Vagrant entirely
        I borrow time

Giving in
        finesses giving up

Electing something devouring
        finesses giving up
                superbly

Now this universe at large has lost an I
        I
                locates

Seeing invents
    otherwise anywhere
        is a same nonplace

Nonsense errant
    makes a bid to submerge it all

Tumult seiges each boulder

Assiduous its breakers
    maul each island

Buggerall stops still

Three quarters of an age
    I devoted to sloth and worry
        nearabout dead

Whenever I do halfwise
    that dreadful I O U
        closely held
            grows

No rockdove says I

No pelican

A cumbrance
    for voyagers
        lined in a V

Being human makes traveling
    harder with some reason
        if it compounds with becoming
        pleasures worth
            just traveling for

The variable I
    rehearses values
        that like to approach constant X

Character happens while selves attend other urgencies
    and the form that unseen X is
        intuited from vividly drawn dreams
            mind projects on the odd daytime seascape
            barely noticed produces
            the I Steady Stand
                or phantom I am

X
    saturates

Meanwhile I walk miles graced
    with circling gulls
        storks lofted
            garnering
                of the very island

The very searocks exhale X

Most truth lies
    but in strict rhythm lies
        accuracy in a way
            now arbitrary
            now direct

Measure is action

So this metrician
    X says I am
        squares the spheres
          we hear
            every footfall
            centers

———————— 0 ————————

Inland for a sight
    climb passages
        reciting a history
            each mountain bespeaks a piece of

Orogenies do

Narrative yearns
    to continue
        as geography
            is never done

Expansion a century a digit
    has charms even the wholly frantic
        educated gradually to
            might apprehend

Not simply

——————— 0 ———————

X
    I say
        can

Rocks may

Water says
    counting enchants it

Each figure trains waves to a new hypnotic ease I have
    copied painfully
        while I confirmed
            when I seize X
                X eludes

Cuchulain
    hews the sea

Waves
    trouble at nothing

Yet taking scant thought
    water
        toothless
            gnaws senseless a shoreline
            rawly new

Possessed of a brainpan
    facing X
        I blinked
            yes
                grasping a mischance for it
                facing X I forbore
                mymisself and I

Known X
    I imagined
        would lose vitality

Suppose that this heresy be now finally abandoned
    supposing dinner is frankly more startling after having
        starved for years a hopeless abnegant quite tightly
            woven in weblets of self dominion espousing
                a by no stretch universal law
                relieved
                I remember now

I a patchwork from wayonback
    I an epiphenom emergent
        for the moment
            compact for the moment am
            hard work

Suited labor charms
    fervor
        past due

Peripaty counts

As a day convolves
    this clockwise pace around the perimeter
        turns on an edgy craving for mastery
            I recognize

Roaming

As a century convolves
    peramble counts

Songlines
    tune
        the travels

So rhythms thicken

Timed for walkabout by a skysign
    I measure myself by milestone for a roadway
        sandal leather takes on the waywiser
            with nearly nothing left unproven I discover
            this merely walking making living
                seriously
                    fine

Mused
    I say so

———————— 0 - 0 ————————

BLOOD STRUTS LORDLIER
    I do believe
        a body given to taking
            joy where bidden

Fortunes in delight pervade anyplace sense awakens
    example
        a guy with an octopus
            turns seawall
                through thorough thwacking
                    tender

Elsewhere
    a rooster too dimwit for morning I suppose
        blithely hollers at a blue heaven overhead
            lust loud

Splendoes

I am an eary gathering
    quiet
        and loud too

A boat passes
    laden with wayfarers
        steam sounding forth his initial O

Oomph

Echoing pulsation of an echoing pulsation
    voices vitulate broadcast
        on every timeworn frequency
            to get their word in

A helpfully undefined limit
    namely I
        f of X
            am listening

So a quodlibet
    begins

Creation
    pushes back

The next cape I navigate
    a coast brilliant etcetera
        a new manner of arranging reality
            repeats that nothing
                masters a day

Impatient
    prodigity rounds

Wryly
    a fraction escapes

Mindful of X
    I set down whichever dimension
        whichever magnitude
            whichever direction suggests the vectors
                of veritably pilgrim progress

Most theolatry bullshits about X

Since doctrinal middens are a pitfall
    out of courtesy
        X eludes

Hindsight
    traces out
        a rambling
            bound
                territory round

It maps
    this value beginning with
        three point one four
            wooing expansion

Fabulous day

An ardent toil of
    prowl it is
        too

Plenties of hours
    and for each word
        twenty trancing steps

The heart is speech
    a perimeter
        and I
            a rational diameter
          I address X

O

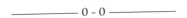 0 - 0

AND I CAN COMPASS STEPPING OUT
    sideways without being an untoward outaline
        faring paths findable
          between wants
          and has to

Wherever
    and whenever I need to

Behind a hillock
    a further hillock arises
        series

extending I feel
endless and

Not right naturally
interior is bound and thus
reachable

Just as Odyssean cursive trips trace some Aegean bestiary
showing how a π might designate
areas easily as limiting curves for divagate argument
so the lines any venture overland between hills describes
all meander about a
peninsula minus isthmus
finally spelling
a babbling drawl tending
Ithacan
homeward

After all
if I signify
I do it before thinking

Chance
choose a way

———— 0 ————

A HUMDINGER
of another stairway
notated mutely
begins C D E
ascending
agile intervals

Logarithm of a scalar
step
up

A monotonic goatbell
    somewhere off
      confirms

Harmonial
    scads of birds
      entitle me

I

Beyond where this hillside climb declines
    giving way to gentler geodesic tangents
      beyond where indulging the sloped
        a craze
          has its setbacks
            I plodding or lightly
              gravitate toward
                desiring to fly

How

I delectate
    going to

And going too

A peculiar piece of highblown rustic rhetoric ricochets aimlessly about various
    heights the better to be heard overabove headwinds that a sun stiffens
      hazarding a no less fruitless descent to a muddled echoing depth
        to validate the most fuckwit theophany I ken
          a dance I dance
            quite elegant with practice
            quite regular
              to walk to talk
                being
                  what I heard

Memory
    producing music
        reabsorbs music

Fanfares no orchestra belts out
    and I a player
        resonate around a network of earshot
            focusing every nerve
            rewarded
                spirally receptive

Valleys
    sound

Listening minutely for
    instance I saunter
        along this saddle
           all yawning ears
              noting what melodizes the formulary
              for X
                  economies of scale aside

Stride

Rite

———————— 0 ————————

ATTENTION
    is telling
        measure

A needle
    seeking X
        I pay attention

———————— 0 ————————

Villagers abruptly
    this rambling
        populate
            in kind

I go fumbling
    among palatals and velars
        a barbar

Old women darken
    the benches

Donkeys
    loudly abound

O

They radiate X

A sentence I construct from my halfassed lexic hoard earns gestures toward
    a planetree shielded whitewash cool minute taverna
        inside looking suitable for someone
            more sore footweary even than foreseen
                to drink amply and appease clamoring stomach
                    happily with company if mutely
                        mouthing each forkful
                          O

Good

Good heavens
    mercy how late things have gotten to

Goodbyes

With speech hooked together
    just
        we build farewells

Ritual exchanges bind everybody
   I am persuaded
      all via a few
         rococo
            singing phrases

In timefast
   mouthworn formulas
      naturally
         I speak an I

With similar grace
   am I spoken to

After speech
   guestgift beside
      amazed

No shit

Seven apricots

The angelist
   a child

A messenger for which
   X I be sworn
      who now reselect
      my lone way

——————— 0 ———————

ALL THESE PATHS
   untimely decline
      except this

It goes lilting into cloudless heaven
    like someone who is chosen for gallantry
       a road I gleefully recognize
         as company to esteem

With an oblate afternoon ascending so
    to optimal parabolic climax
      slowing steadily
        as now
           takes hold
              playing gravitas
                  I follow its camber

—————— 0 ——————

FOLLOWING
    and lost
      I startle at a glance
        what I in a hastiness perceived as wild
         paths resemble alleys
         and I climb

Old

To evacuate coasts
    a ratsnest of murderous pirates
      they built these steep streets

Eleven hundred year anamnesis
    sheathes the impacted walls

Round town helically from plain upthrust
    revolved solid
      churches strewn
        countless as houses elsewhere
       numbering
         every annual saintsday

Boulevard
    up springs
        as S

Traffic
    thinkably
        crowded aloft

Abandoned now

As centuries press forth
    out of X
        X builds again
            the town
                once
                    realities resorted equally to

To decades quiet lanes
    peoplings retend

Or not
    either bond
        haunting

Either mortar holds fast
    tenacious guarantee
        a T buttjoint coupling normally
            I likewise fit
                just another transient
                    knowing whither bound and
                        where finger plucks the thread
                        stretched lifelong

However long or lopped short
    ever it loves to vibrate urgently
        tensed to pitch
            draws a notation

                              a likeness
                          a ghostly shape visible like
                      hollow village
                          in emptiest readiness

Desertion
        revives silence
            resting lightly
                on hearths
                    perfected for sleeping

————————— 0 - 0 —————————

WHATEVER X BUILDS
        time empties

Enough

————————— 0 —————————

I RECKON I KEEP GOING
        on some plenitude I construct
            as a present
                and as a habitat
                    as a daft diagram
                        pointed to one south

I find I have lost a carefully ordered
        and quite nicely balanced daily mind recently
            I expect I was giving X a nasty asspain
                for plans no worse given up I see
                    for mere delight
                        which finally gets
                            a complete free pseudopod over things
                                excepted only the farthest shore
                                    as the end of the itinerary

Delight now awakening like a hard sun
    all the body dread made antlike
        recalls Aeacus
           by Zeus
              a raised myrmidon cohort
                  to yield a manifold companion outright
                    and later render grandsons
                like Achilles
                  worth being
                    roused by

Feelingly surprised as a butterfly to be an I
    Aeginant
        body is tickled
           in every sense

As every inch of nerve
    itches rigorous
        whatever circuit sorely charged
          I inhabit
            persuades

Very temporary
    this engine

I wonder where
    say
        wild horses wander nowadays

This planetary peepshow
    arranges itself
        to mystify me
          and to provide
            sometimes
              a through composed
              anthem

Steadily since morning creation puts out
　　　radiance for radiance
　　　　　as someone willingly driven without
　　　　　　　resentful scruple should expect
　　　　　　　　whenever X gets mixed into I

———————— 0 ————————

AFTERNOON GOING FOR CLIMBING
　　climbing the central eminence
　　　ascent for assent

Amazement
　　rises

Stride shortens

———————— 0 ————————

SURELY
　　what is up
　　　　ahead I go
　　　　　　bound to

Every I
　　I imagine
　　　　and construct
　　　　　　in projected sections
　　　　　　　here
　　　　　　　　directly
　　　　　　　　　completes itself

Becoming what I do
　　becoming what
　　　sojourns
　　　　becoming harder to locate
　　　　　justifies this lanky rhumba

Step by step
   I
        instructs broken trail
           in mounting
             steep

Up it
   is X

Nobody except X
   a dwelling
      spoken for

Myself looking down this
   no kidding
      thousand cubits of it

And certainly a knowledge that redefines what knows

Once offered
   I is the present I was
      forever promised
         island centering summit

Whereupon these loaned and lifted eyes con leagues
   I enumerate a horizon
      an infinite perfect line broken without visible damage
         upon random known islands
            named islands and recounted islets of this
              I see
                stranger homeworld

Studious toward every footnote
   jot or tittle
      rapt sight ingathers
         geography which reflects
           a day

                        too
                    declining

All beckons
    downhill

Ah
    orogasm
        eases
            shoreward

———————— 0 ————————

PANEGYRIC
    unwinding talk
        praise
            falls overall
                easily down

Various ordinary graphemes
    enter a no longer terribly hard formal contract
        and forthwith unawares
            the light of naked gratitude
                comes dancing

Wavelight reflects
    an order
        obscured
            as no others do

Order is an urge
    resisted
        sparingly
            best

History derides an ending
    nothing a landscape does insists remotely
       on ending
          puzzling what
             delights in ending

A good measure
    begins
       revolving clockwise

Revolving

An ageold ache

A sun arises and intrigues some mind
    and finally goes under water
       yes

Heart

Number measures it

The most satisfied estate of words to find
    takes a pattern from somewhere
       and assembles windfalls inside
          since a body has a mind
             to indemnify likewise

Repeating
    a beginning

Urchin grips
    epochally
       to rocks

Diligence can decline
    to be a wholly worthless burden

with barely a shrug
a small miracle

Attention
mirabile dictu
fulfills the peculiar
wistful name
I

Where attention returns
mirabile frigging dictu
generally there amazement equally rewakes
as listening
engaged
takes over faculties
switched otherwise
off

A bellow a roaring laugh and posthaste an ecstatic wave speaks lethally
a ten syllable of itself
ordained before sunlight yet hitherto always anywhere
unheardof with no prudent prelude
with a total noisy impudence affirming
a wondrous crass grand certainty
as large as life likes
shadowing forth
how hereafter every
solitaire will
say I

This darkening deposited sealand
as light as time leaves
shimmers

Twilight runs under porcelain sealight
filling in hollows and hiding hill feet
before spreading along sealanes

               like invading pirate sails
                   the nightmen
                       and taking finally the summit
                           so as to finish up neatly

Panegyric amplifies
    a so long
        solong

Minutely

Cries O
    to know
        how anything vanishes
            into the wolflight

Then cries O to know
    when a day begins
        about what precisely
            anybody should be already
                worrying

Looking backwards
    looking forward
        a lucky number
            withholds
                a full and final reckoning
                    seriously teasing
                        closure

from MORNING NOON & NIGHT

ORRERY

By the window, the bucket, in the bucket, the mop
and a foot of gray water. The old man picks up the bucket
and carries it to another corner. Hours trickle down.
The old woman comes in and moves it
closer to the door. In the late afternoon the old man
nudges it with his foot right up to the threshhold,
coddling the mop's handle upright to lean on the jamb.
The water eddies slowly, slows, can barely be seen
moving. With elaborate precision the sun rolls down the sky
to the bottom, and covers itself with sea. Moon comes up,
goes over, the old man and the old woman snore
in turn, like the pistons of an old, old engine.
At midnight the son comes home drunk. No no—
he says—he steps nimbly over the bucket—
then turns and kicks it into the garden.
Earth and the water darken each other, with no one to see it.

                                                    15.VI.99

THAT LAND

The stalks of bamboo tick together like claws
all night; the child wakes again and again,
partway, to think about a foreign country. Beside the bed
the parents sit silent, and the grandparents and great-grandparents,
and their parents—rings of chairs. The child
wakes again just enough to think, Everything in that land
wants to eat me; but the child isn't afraid.
The bamboo stays outside the window,
like the almond tree, whose flowers seem to fill the room.

                                                    15.VI.99

TUREEN

The plates, scrubbed, go back to their rack,
the cups to theirs. Then someone hungers, thirsts,
a flurry of activity, then sitting around dirty.

Night spills in and soap comes, and the sponge.
Back in the cupboard, the plates on one side, upright,
cups upside down on the other, the air is stifling,
there is practically nothing to do
but dream of an heroic ideal, a tureen, insurgent,
or an earthquake. As the weeks decay,
a cup flings itself to fragments on the floor;
a plate, cracked, disappears for good;
and every so many months, new, familiar faces
arrive in time for the holidays.

16.VII.99

FASCINATION

He buys a glass mask; now under the water he can see.
He buys frogfeet to swim to what he sees, and a tube
so he can breathe. After a while he buys a spear
with three barbs, and though he draws the line at a gun with elastics,
now he can impale what he sees. Everything stays away then,
of course, but he is fascinated by his new powers,
he carries his things everywhere in a canvas bag,
and some nights he gets up secretly and in the dark he puts it all on
and gazes at his watery reflection in the mirror of the sideboard.
Everyone sleeps, and the soft flopping of his feet through the house
barely disturbs the mice.

17.VI.99

ALL WAYS

Half-light, wolf-light, I have walked to this bench
—he says—ten months a year every evening. The same
bench over the same sea, the same islands on the skyline.
The identical moon, more or less. The star of evening again,
and later the many stars. All ways the same—he says—
except the wayward ways of men, and that except me, my ways remain
unalterable, though not eternal. They say this stone
I tap my cane upon is turning wildly in space, in place
yet also all over! and I believe it. Look at that cloud,
you'd think it was a mountain if you hadn't always seen the mountains.

17.VI.99

IN SHREDS

Here's that wind again, he says.
It puts feathers and pillowcases on the sea
and sprays the sheets hung on lines over the alley.
It hangs the seagulls still and drives the doves backwards.
The trees would tell you which way it blows
if you were deaf and insensible. It ventilates
the skirts of the widows one way uphill
and the other way down. If I had nails and a hammer
I'd teach it to sit still. (The wind carries
words away in shreds.) But then—he says—
I suppose it would rain.

18.VI.99

ACCIDENTS

In the lot behind the restaurant sits his crumpled car,
just as he said. He lives over the restaurant.
His dog lies on the cool front seat, on her long chain, chin
on the steering wheel, and growls. He went over a cliff
near the next town, tumbled dozens of meters
down the shore. He has a new motorbike
and also a new puppy who chews his shoes, or pees in them,
it wasn't clear, it wouldn't have been clear at all
except that dogs do only so many things to shoes,
only so many things happen to cars near the sea to crumple them,
and people tell only some kinds of stories about their lives.

19.VI.99

HOLLOWS

Moon in the day, never the sun at night.
Water inland, never land long under water
because it isn't called that any more.
In hollows in the rocks, pockets of salt.
Summer coming to term in locusts' dozing.
Cat in the open window, wrapped, asleep.
In a bed, in the afternoon, a man in a woman.
Fire inside the lantern. Roots in earth.

19.VI.99

CROWD CONTROL

At the edge of town whole families plash like seals
on the lip of the sea. A child digs sand in handfuls
from the beach and flings it into the water. The waves
keep smoothing everything. Groups of mostly naked people
stand around gossiping, now and then one sits down
to cool off and stands up dripping. A father flings his son
over and over into the air. The young parade, the old paddle.
On a bench beside the beach, a man in a suit,
a man in a suit and tie,
and beside the bench, a sign: Forbidden the Swimming of Dogs.

20.VI.99

SORITES

The use of the moon is unknown. The weight of the moon
is negligible. The light of the moon guides the evolution of moths.
The evolution of anxiety has never ceased nor hesitated.
The anxiety of moths is palpable and strict. Start again.
The moon rises during the day so as to see what is going on.
Start again. O moon—he begins—o moon . . .
The difference between the moon at night and the moon during the day
is the whole measure of the brilliance of the sky. The measure
of what is lost in a day with no moon
is the weight of the moth's wing
to the moth.

20.VI.99

THE APOTHEOSIS

The lamb in the window has arrived at the height of self-absorption.
Like an invalid whom everything bothers, everything bores except illness,
it has perfected concentration on an ideal. Divested
of that greasy burr-clotted fleece its soul approaches spotlessness
like the sheet of slick paper under its high-hung head,
only five or six small gouts. And occasions of sin diminish swiftly.
Its heart is pure and empty, at hand in a small bowl.
A woman stops to admire the lamb—more than admire, to contemplate
its forthcoming transfiguration over a softly flickering bed of coals
and subsequent transubstantiation into her large family.

21.VI.99

DOVES

Twenty-three doves stand calmly on the top wire,
every coloration the island knows, classic white
through ur-beige to banded and mottled anyhow.
Below them on the third wire of five, four sparrows fidget.
Suddenly, wings snapping, a report like a small gun, the doves
leap into the air together. A minute of panic, baseless
to judge from their ready settling back on the same wire, same
catalogue positions, but too much for the sparrows, who flee.
A good shot could pick off twenty-two in half an hour
before the last one caught on, but it would be demeaning.

21.VI.99

PLANNING

At the harbor all the passengers who are not yet passengers
inhabit the benches as slowly as they can, they comb their hair,
refold newspapers and eat nuts. Acres of concrete reflect the sun.
A boat comes in, but it's only a fishing boat, nets half-full of creatures
beyond boredom. The wind picks up, dies down, for the sake of incident.
Should a startling juxtaposition, a telling counterpoint, come in?
But the boat still isn't here and fancying doesn't bring it, not talk
nor narrative serendipity. No—he says—what brings the boat eventually
will be cooperative enterprise, to construct clocks, to define sea-lanes,
to organize ticket-sellers and second mates and underwriters
and yes, loads of people to sit around providing expectation.
The dreams prancing behind their vacant stares are of no account.

21.VI.99

A VOCATION

In a row the baker lays out the loaves to rise in the dark
under their coverlets of cheesecloth like babies in bassinets
or the first tidying after a massacre. The baker leaves
for his small sleep and the cat comes in to count the loaves
and to pray disinterestedly for their ascension. Her meditation
is on the mice whose susurrus inside the ceiling
and back of the bales of paper behind the furnace
and along the narrow alleys in walls

reminds her of the sea, or rather when she hears the sea,
sotto voce, it reminds her of mice. She thinks
it's the sound that helps the moonlit sea to rise.
In the miracle, the bread the dead resemble multiplies.

22.VI.99

IN THE HANDS OF THE BREEZES

In the hands of the breezes doors all over the house
open and close in turn, at random, swaying slightly
or slamming with a final report. Nothing. The breezes seem
to want something they can't find, perhaps can't even remember,
and they search the same corners over and over, trying,
moving light things around in the same eddies, dust-
cats and dust-mice, a receipt from the pharmacy, a petal
blown in from the bougainvillea, the vine the breezes shake feebly,
futilely, not even knowing what question to ask.

23.VI.99

VISIBLE END

The pile of cut brush by the garden wall. The secret of the martyr
woven into the shroud. The wires hung from pole to pole with no
visible end. The stone centered on the pier. The hour
fastened to the four corners of the table. The hand on the table,
closed, its back in the air. The dog led down the road by odors.
The mention of a certain name. The four feet of the chair.
The station of the sun over the clock tower. The air
entrained by all the rest of the air, more than a fish in school,
more than a cormorant in the dotted line of an arrow.
The arrow, halfway past
halfway there.

23.VI.99

NOT ONE

The two—he says—are distinct and inseparable
like the color and the motion of an olive grove
or the pitch and timbre of a voice lingering over a name,
not like sky and sea on a hazy day when islands

and boats seem to float in a false position. Sometimes—he says—
they overlap like the two hands in the lap of an old woman in church
or the thought and word and deed of an honorable man,
not like fig leaves over the first offenders' suddenly private parts.
Never, though, are they one, any more than your two feet,
or your flesh and blood.

23.VI.99

ON THE BEACH

The dog lies sleeping on the beach in the late afternoon, waves
thrashing uphill nearly to her nose. She starts awake
at a bit of blown plastic, settles back
with concentrated attention on her face. She is dreaming
of flying, borne over the seaspray, legs ever on the stretch.
She dreams she is a ship, the very good ship Dog, with a crew of men
to caulk and trim her daily. She dreams the sea is a cat, a very
large cat, better ignored, fortunately confined. On the beach
the noise is amazing, waves on waves, red light poring over them.

24.VI.99

UNACCOUNTABLE

The heart of man—he says—is a mailbox dying of curiosity.
The soul entrusts it with the inscrutable. Our own houses
stand agape at our audacity. We baffle the sea.
Everything the hand of man lets fall is perfectly unlike
everything other, even and especially when made in imitation.
We astounded the gods when we had gods. Every day—he says—
I surprise myself, don't you? Look at these books, this garden,
that cannon in the square under the marble soldier.

24.VI.99

CROCODILE

The boy on the back of the motorbike clutches in one hand
a green inflated crocodile as big as he is, upright, with handles,
and his father in the other. Wind whistles through the beast's teeth.
The swallows darting over the road veer off sharply.
The very sea reels in terror, or mock terror, it doesn't

signify. The earth rolls backward under the wheels like anything.
And the dog that took out after them, the prize of its young life,
recedes, no bigger than a mouse, and then a flea.

25.VI.99

Egg Salad

What a destiny—he says—for an embryo: all set
to become a hen, a rooster, who knows, filched and bundled
with eleven others in a paper sack; subjected to terminal
thermal insult, roiling heat then running cold; opened
flake by flake to the light like the soul of a prophet;
then diced in a low bowl; mashed; bound and thickened
with mayonnaise and a fierce forkful of mustard. Salt.
A life too strange for plot, a death too delicious for words.

25.VI.99

Colossus

Between two fingers of the hand outstretched a star.
Between the next the paring of a moon. Next, night.
The palm is full of light. The arm a dark road that goes home.
The prominences of the body overflow with brightness
and its recesses give brightness places to go still.
The feet grip down on rock, balancing, balancing.
When the face turns to face north it meets the wind
riding, massed, down from the mountains, and the eye
only blinks. One thin cloud hangs from the roof
and the whole cave of the world is filled
with the commentary of the sea.

26.VI.99

Ticket

I love the moment at the ticket window—he says—
when you are to say the name of your destination, and realize
that you could say anything, the man at the counter
will believe you, the woman at the counter
would never say No, that isn't where you're going,
you're going where you always go. Or to be sure

you could buy a ticket for one place and go to another,
less far along the same line. Suddenly you would find yourself
— he says—in a locality you've never seen before,
where no one has ever met you and you could say your name
was anything you like, nobody would say No,
that isn't you, this is who you are. It thrills me every day.

26.VI.99

THE COLLECTOR

Down among the fishcrates and plastic bottles, among the searocks,
down among splintered bamboo and mayonnaise caps and cuttlebones,
there have to be—he said—statistically speaking
the tailbones of a mermaid; whitening daintily,
curved and socketed like intaglio in ivory. They lie still linked
in a crevice between these yellow blocks of shattered cliff. I know it, I can
see it, and I search. And nobody—he said—
nobody else will stick to it long enough.

26.VI.99

CLEAR

Clear as the sea here is—he says—it's hard to see
what people are doing with their nether limbs,
and this is the first origin of the mermaids; though afterwards
they learned to lay eggs of themselves, like frogs, large single eggs
that hatch out on the sea foam in the sun, the hair already
flowing-long on the nymph as on the fully formed imago.
A man in the next village had one of these eggs—out of water
they perish and are preserved—and it was half-clear
like amber. Unfortunately it was destroyed during the war.
But I myself—he says—have heard them calling
as I lay at sea at night under the deck of my nodding boat.

27.VI.99

CORNER

She moves down the rows of her long shop,
turning and watering, trimming and fluffing up,
naming her charges in a Latin long grafted on Greek,

and comes to a tremendous scarlet blossom
sprung from the corner of a green barrel
like a cloche on the head of a Martian, she says.
Desert succulents—she bursts out—that's all we are,
desert succulents, half thorns,
we store up, we store up, and once a year we wave these
frantic signals at all the pollinators in the world.

27.VI.99

THE MOUNTAIN IN THE MIDDLE

The mountain in the middle could be watching
all its children from bowl to brim, fishing, bargaining,
making rolls and change and babies, swatting goats,
and the goats, the bees, the boats, the trees, all the perched churches,
the chalky limestone north and pumice south, the lesser crags,
the seven valleys in their loveliness, out to its own
very fringes which the wavelets lick—but the mountain
leans back its sunstruck head and loses
its gaze in total blue.

29.VI.99

OFFERING

The salt is on the table, and in the bread, and in every mouthful of sea.
Salt glistens among rocks above high tide, it stings
in the eyes of the divers and the bites of insects, it sticks
skin to skin in siesta and films every seaward surface of glass.
Its savor is in no danger, its word is on every tongue.
On the hills the goats lick it from their own coats.
It tans the hides of the old, beginning when they're young.
Here's a good pinch—he said—take it,
press it between your fingers, rub it into your palm with your thumb,
blow it into the air, it sparkles all the way to the ground.
That's what nobody can live without.

29.VI.99

FACULTIES

The empty drawer in the chest standing three-legged beside the road
hangs out in the sun, filling slowly. It smells of camphor
and salt. The other drawers are closed, one locked. Junk.
The wood inside the open drawer, color of dry grass, color of summer,
has begun to recall so well how it felt to be a branch
that a sparrow flits down to perch, to peek inside with one eye.
Under the chest, in shade a cat waits. The sparrow knows.
Slowly the stuff in the other drawers is forgetting everything.

1.VII.99

STEPWISE

Right hand steadies itself on rock, rock rests
harder on ledge, ledge leans back
that much more on mountain. Left foot feels
for step, instep curls into place, pressed
into mountain. Eye fixes everything
one at a time. Time steps
delicately over stones,
leading. Goat-time, bell-time.
The sun herds it. Left hand, shielding,
frees the eyes from time to time for horizon,
which circles, excited like a dog but
at the speed of light.

1.VII.99

A CERTAIN HOUR

At a certain hour the sun
quite tightly yet so gently hardly a hair's betrayed
grasps the back of the neck and dismounts the skull. The brain,
like a cat of any age plucked by the scruff, entranced,
suffused, forgets the elaborations scheduled by its proprietor
and becomes an intimate of the day, which is enormous, of great depth
and total certainty. So loudly that it bypasses the ear entirely,
the sun speaks its one tremendously long word into the manifold
folds of the brain so that for a moment they exfoliate
like the elephant's fan ear or the photon sail of a hypership,

a couple of square meters of concentration.
Everything is quite, quite clear. Then while the sun averts its gaze
behind a momentary cloud, the brain repacks itself and assumes
some of its former dignity, the regalia of its intent.

1.VII.99

LIBATION

The clean-up man has come into his hour, his own
because everyone else has left it. He carries the tables into the back
and piles the chairs on them, opening the whole front to the sidewalk;
and there with his reiterate broom, little by little,
he causes to accumulate, or he accumulates,
what others dispersed. He won't look until he's finished,
until he's restored the chairs and tables, until the moon has set.
Under the last lamp he has left lit, he pores
over the fruits of his work: the seventy-nine cigarette butts
and six whole cigarettes; the three coins and a small bill folded in thirds;
the tickets for the boat, all cancelled; both halves of a torn map.
One good push and it's all down the gutter, except the bill and cigarettes
and two of the coins.

3.VII.99

SYZYGY

Rain and the idea of rain stroll arm in arm up the coast.
Who cares what anybody thinks? They could tear off
their different kinds of clothes and leap into the sea,
disporting. They could lie down together in a church.
If they were made they were made for each other. If they had families
their families would bury idols to put them right. Under the moon's light
the sea lies under their conjoined ministrations calmed,
all its larger projects dissolved in their millioning.
They love each other more perfectly than you. They have
no secret, they are a secret. No one can see them both at the same time.

3.VII.99

ORDER IN DISORDER

From one table after another stare the same woman and boy
in the same blank-faced postures denoting grief suspended,
over the same caption in three or four languages. On paper
what surrounds them varies, in differing maelstroms they stand still
staring. Gulls feint and squabble among the awnings,
the tops of masts nod like a forest of violin bows,
the intratabular and intertabular diplomacy of the waterfront
is constructive, is promising, and the woman and the boy
stare together past the glances of people and gulls into the white sky.

4.VII.99

THE RESPONSIBILITY

It wasn't what we planned—she said—but we have it here, stiff
and accusatory, as if it were ours, or our fault. We have it,
arms and legs and all, and these few clothes for it, which we can't
get it into. We should leave it outside until it behaves better.
We have a name for it on this paper. We don't see the use of it, nor do
the children any more. The people across the road have one too,
what are things coming toward? We found a box almost big enough,
if we could fold it up. There's a space behind the lemon tree maybe
big enough for the box. They gave us time, till evening. The children
are tired of playing with it, they go off to touch the butts
of the soldiers' rifles and run away. The soldiers are all right, they're older.

4.VII.99

STAY

Under the walls the dead. Under the dreams
dreams of the dead. Over the far hill
the acid, purifying light of early morning.
Taste in the mouth of stale time, still.
In the long brick shed the sheep and chickens
stay legs folded gazing quietly through the air.
The dead lie under our walls to hold them up.
What would we do without them? We'll never know.
The animals, snug, know better than to build.

6.VII.99

THE DOOR

A door from somewhere, off its hinges, across trestles for painting,
its knocker tilted up to keep out of it, handle a green
brass island in the fresh brown, glares with what authority it can
under the circumstances at the impertinent open sky.
The idea that anyone can be on either side of it
makes it sweat. As for the jamb left to its own
totally naive devices, the thought is not to be endured.
The street in front of the door empties for a few hours,
fills again for the evening bustle, all those shoes tap by,
and no one all night will knock.

6.VII.99

READY

The cedar weighs an extra hundred pounds with dew.
In a haze the hills are still half awake.
On the phone poles the crows practice the flap-and-caw,
and the wind runs its fingertips through everything tousled,
everything sleep-matted and not spruce for day.
The hedgehog doesn't count, just now bedded back down,
but the lizard, frozen on its already hot rock, stands prepared
to take on any demoiselle thrown at it, the old man
on the bench in the square has nearly made up his mind to walk,
and the butterflies are going crazy around each other over the oregano.

8.VII.99

MISPLACED

The woman at the last table thumbs through an album:
the previous week: mountain, mountain, sunset, sunset, sunset,
friends, more friends, sea, sea, sea, goat, herd of goats,
man riding a horse off a cliff into the sea, sunset,
sea. She sighs and sets it down and sips her tea.
He's sitting at the next table, the next to last, his hair dripping
as it always will, as will his horse,
who stands nearby with baleful eyes,
but she avoids their gaze as deftly as the waiter.
It was only her camera, only a moment's notice . . .

8.VII.99

GLIMPSE

Sleep—sleep for such as us—he says—
is a page of words stretching in all directions
without end, although our ability to sample it,
nap by nap even over a whole life, is circumscribed.
The wonder is that any time we are set down on it
we are set down in a new place, or almost every time,
there's barely moment enough to figure out which way
the words are running before we're taken up again
like divers letting their last air buoy them back above,
yet we come back regularly with quite marvelous stories
gleaned in a glimpse. It is also striking to me—he says—
that though we hear from each other of familiar passages,
we almost never meet anyone there, except the dead.
I suppose it's just that there are so many more of them.

9.VII.99

Index of Titles

About the Author

CHARLES O. HARTMAN has published six collections of poems and three critical books: *Free Verse, Jazz Text,* and *Virtual Muse*. He is Poet in Residence at Connecticut College, and plays jazz guitar.

Ahsahta Press

Ahsahta Press

MODERN AND CONTEMPORARY
POETRY OF THE AMERICAN WEST

This book is set in Apollo MT type by Ahsahta Press at Boise State University
and manufactured according to the Green Press Initiative
by Thomson-Shore, Inc.
Cover design by Quemadura.
Book design by Janet Holmes.

AHSAHTA PRESS
2008

JANET HOLMES, DIRECTOR
BREONNA KRAFFT
AMBER NELSON
DAVID SCOTT
NAOMI TARLE
ROSS HARGREAVES, INTERN